# Why Am I a Jew?

# Why Am I a Jew?

Spinoza Revisited

MICHAEL BAUM

RESOURCE *Publications* • Eugene, Oregon

WHY AM I A JEW?
Spinoza Revisited

Copyright © 2022 Michael Baum. All rights reserved. Except for brief quotations in critical publications or reviews, no part of this book may be reproduced in any manner without prior written permission from the publisher. Write: Permissions, Wipf and Stock Publishers, 199 W. 8th Ave., Suite 3, Eugene, OR 97401.

Resource Publications
An Imprint of Wipf and Stock Publishers
199 W. 8th Ave., Suite 3
Eugene, OR 97401

www.wipfandstock.com

PAPERBACK ISBN: 978-1-6667-3099-9
HARDCOVER ISBN: 978-1-6667-2302-1
EBOOK ISBN: 978-1-6667-2303-8

.                                              JANUARY 4, 2022 8:48 AM

I dedicate this book to the memory of Baruch Spinoza
And my four siblings
(The late) Dr. Geoffrey Baum
Professor Harold Baum
(The late) Professor J David Baum
and
my little sister Linda Kingsley
Between them they encouraged my critical thinking and acted as sounding boards for my spiritual development

# Contents

*Prologue* | ix

| | | |
|---|---|---|
| CHAPTER 1 | A Very Small Spider in a Very Large Book | 1 |
| CHAPTER 2 | Was the Spider Created or Did it Evolve? | 5 |
| CHAPTER 3 | Are We Looking for God in the Wrong Place? | 9 |
| CHAPTER 4 | Development of Ethical Code beyond a Belief in the Supernatural | 18 |
| CHAPTER 5 | The Good, the Bad and the Ugly of Monotheistic Religions | 22 |
| CHAPTER 6 | A Question of Community | 43 |
| CHAPTER 7 | Why *Am* I a Jew? | 48 |
| CHAPTER 8 | Circumcision and Kashrut | 72 |
| CHAPTER 9 | Why I Am a Zionist? | 84 |
| CHAPTER 10 | The God of Inner Space | 94 |

CHAPTER 11     Baruch Spinoza I | 105

CHAPTER 12     Spinoza II: A Book Forged in Hell | 112

CHAPTER 13     Faith in Science | 123

CHAPTER 14     My Search for the Divine | 133

*Bibliography* | *143*

*Index* | *147*

# *Prologue*

THIS IS A VERY AMBITIOUS book and at the time of writing I was never sure of completing the task and not even sure how it would end. In other words, I made it up as I went along and much of it surprised me as it appeared in writing. I'm not implying that there was anything supernatural about this process, I don't believe I was taking dictation from above (God forbid) or that there was a muse sitting on my right shoulder, but the book seemed to write itself. Effectively this work attempts to put my beliefs on trial as witness for the defense as I challenge myself, on behalf of the prosecution, to justify myself for those opinions. In this book, I express my opinions on multiple philosophical and religious questions that have challenged all the great thinkers of the past. I am a dilettante and self-taught philosopher but if I see further, it's not so much that I'm standing on the shoulders of giants (*pace* Isaac Newton), it's because I've had to practice their philosophical teachings in my efforts to support and cure my patients facing the existential threat of cancer.

I have been privileged to enjoy more than one career in my long and busy life.

I qualified as a doctor in 1960 and was appointed to my first chair of surgery in 1980 at Kings College London and went on to be appointed Professor of surgery at the Institute of Cancer research in 1990 and then to a chair of surgery at University College London (UCL) in 1997. I retired from my clinical work as a surgeon at the age of 67 but was kept on as a part time non-clinical post with

## PROLOGUE

the title of visiting professor in Medical Humanities at UCL. In that role, I helped set up a new curriculum in the teaching of the humanities to medical students. This involved teaching scientific philosophy, moral philosophy, the psycho-social impact of disease, communication skills, narrative based medicine, the history of medicine, and the role of the performing arts and the visual arts in the practice of medicine. The students took to this novelty in their curriculum, like ducks to water but many of my senior colleagues who had spent their careers isolated in silos, were deeply skeptical.

After my hectic life as a surgeon and a leader of a cancer research group, I found my life as a Professor in the "soft sciences" much less stressful, allowing me the time to develop other interests including philosophy and art.

I set out to write this book to leave a legacy to students and teachers of medical humanities of the future, however as I described above, it took on a life of its own. I seem to have ended up with a dissertation that attempts to unify many different aspects of scholarly discourse that cross boundaries of all the faculties of the Universities that have employed me. C.P. Snow, preempted me in part with his Rede Lecture in 1959, "The Two Cultures and the Scientific Revolution" (Cambridge University Press). I would like to quote from this as follows.

> *Literary intellectuals at one pole-at the other scientists, and the most representative, the physical scientists. Between the two a gulf mutual incomprehension-sometimes hostility and dislike, but most of all a lack of understanding. They have a curious distorted image of each other. Their attitudes are so different that, even on the level of emotion, they can't find much common ground.*

In my lifetime things have greatly improved and the fact that we were able to establish a course in the humanities in the Science faculty at UCL is evidence enough but there has been no reciprocity. I'm unaware of any teaching of the scientific method in the Arts faculties of British universities. The model of harmony I'm trying to compose is multi-dimensional to include the biological sciences, cosmology and the ontology of God!

## PROLOGUE

I start off by describing my encounter with a very small red spider and my awe of the beauty of its structure and its microscopic function. This then sets me off thinking about the meaning of "her" life compared with the meaning of my life and our roles in the complex ecological system of our planet. This is followed by considering the place of mankind in the cosmos but also looking inward at our own microcosm at increasing degrees of magnification.

I then set about trying to explain how all these scientific insights set me off in the ontological search for God. I start off by describing the good, the bad and the ugly sides of religious beliefs and argue that we are looking for "God" in the wrong place. I then try to justify my apparent cognitive dissonance of retaining my Jewish identity whilst denying the existence of a God with the attributes described in the five books of Moses. I argue that we should look for "God" in the infinitely small spaces within ourselves instead of the infinitely large spaces of the universe. My "God" would not mind whether I believed in "him" or not, so long as I practiced my life as I practice my medicine; in a never-ending quest to improve length and quality of life for all those in my orbit in the hope that others would do the same.

Along the way whilst writing this book I was trying to improve my knowledge of the philosophers who wrote on the ontology of God. To my delight, I realized that all my efforts ended up by rediscovering Baruch Spinoza, he reached the same conclusions in the mid 17thC, more than 350 years ago. He got there first, so I dedicate this book to the eternal memory of this humane and much misunderstood man.

# Prologue

**Codicil**

As chance would have it, I end up writing the final version of this manuscript in the days of the great plague of 2020/2021 (The COVID-19 pandemic), so to quote Samuel Johnson:

> *"Depend upon it, sir, when a man knows he is to be hanged in a fortnight, it concentrates his mind wonderfully"*

# Chapter 1

## A Very Small Spider in a Very Large Book

I RECENTLY FINISHED READING a very large book, over 1.0 kg by weight and 866 pages by length.

The book, by Paul Auster, has the intriguing title, 4-3-2-1. It's very long as it is built up from four different narratives about a young boy, Ferguson, growing up to be a young man in the years 1955–1970 in New Jersey, USA. The clever conceit of the book is that it is the same boy in each case yet with four different life trajectories three of which are cut short.

The catalyst that provoked me to write this tract, was a very small bright red spider that shared the book with me. I first noticed the spider when I was on page 365. Initially it looked as if a printed letter had taken on a life of its own, then I thought I was about to experience one of my rare episodes of visual migraine, that is migraine without the headache. The red spot the size of the letter o in this text, then moved into the center of my visual field and came to a halt as if to study me. I was thus able, in return to study the spider in detail. The body was a most beautiful scarlet and it

## Why Am I a Jew?

sprouted 8 tiny exquisitely engineered legs, that started propelling the creature up the page once it realized it had been noticed. This minute miracle of creation, perfect in structure, design and function, eventually disappeared into the space behind the two-inch-deep spine of the book. I never saw that little beast again, but she gave me pause for thought.

What is the point of a spider's existence either from an arachno-centric or an anthropo-centric point of view? Does a spider think, does a spider experience pleasure or fear or is it simply a turbulent spaghetti-soup of instincts? Does a spider wonder about the meaning of life or is it up to me to wonder on her behalf? Is there even a spidery concept of an almighty being, that rewards good behavior by blowing insects into its web? Come to think of it; in the food chain are there any insects small enough to be captured and ingested by this spider of near microscopic proportions? For that matter what is the point of my existence in the greater scheme of things? In cosmological terms, there is not much difference in my size and the size of my spider. In terms of the ratio in height between the spider and me is about 1/ 2,000 that's equivalent to the ratio in height between me at the Matterhorn! But that is only $2 \times 10^3$ cm order of magnitude compared with $10^{30}$ cm order of magnitude out to the cosmic horizon of the expanding universe.

It is commonplace to see God's work in the cosmos as illustrated by the last paragraph of Stephen Hawking's best seller, *A Brief History of Time*: *"There may be only one complete unified theory that is self-consistent and allow the existence of structures as complicated as human beings who can investigate the laws of the universe and ask about the nature of God. If we find the answer to that, it would be the ultimate triumph of human reason, for then we would know the mind of God"*.[1] I enjoy that same sense of awe from the study of inner space rather than outer space. Consider me as a relatively intact though somewhat worn-out member of the species *Homo Sapiens*. Let me indulge myself with a little introspection about the structures of my "inner space". My body is organized as a hierarchical or holistic structure. Biological "holons" are self-regulating

---

1. Hawking S, *A brief history of time: from big bangs to black holes*, 256.

## A Very Small Spider in a Very Large Book

open systems which display both the autonomous properties of wholes and the dependent properties of parts. The basic building block of life must be a sequence of DNA, that codes for a specific protein. These DNA sequences or genes are organized within chromosomes forming the human genome. The chromosomes are packed within the nucleus with an awe-inspiring degree of miniaturization. The nucleus is a holon looking inwards at the genome and outwards at the cytoplasm of the cell. The cell is a holon that looks inwards at the proteins which guarantee its structure and function contained within its plasma membrane, and at the energy transduction pathways contained within the mitochondria which produce the fuel for life. As a holon, the cell looks outwards at neighboring cells of a self-similar type which may group together as glandular elements, but the cellular holon also enjoys crosstalk with cells of a different developmental origin communicating by touch through tight junctions, or by the exchange of chemical messages via short-lived paracrine polypeptides. These glandular elements and stromal elements group together as a functioning organ which is holistic in looking inwards at the exquisite functional integrity of itself, and outwards to act in concert with the other organs of the body. This concert is orchestrated at the next level in the holistic hierarchy through the neuroendocrine/immunological control mediated via the hypothalamic–pituitary axis, the thyroid gland, the adrenal gland, the endocrine glands of sexual identity, and the lympho-reticular system that can distinguish self from non-self. Even this notion of self is primitive compared with the next level up on the hierarchy where the person exists in a conscious state somewhere within the cerebral cortex, with the mind as the great unexplored frontier.

Let me now re-focus on the structure and function of my (and your) "basic building blocks".

Watson and Crick discovered the structure of DNA in 1953 and subsequent biological scientists have come up with mind-boggling statistics as awe inspiring as those related to cosmology. DNA is made up of a double helix nucleotide. It has been estimated that our body is made up of $6 \times 10^{12}$ meters of DNA. Each nucleotide contains a phosphate group, a sugar group and a nitrogen base. The four types of nitrogen bases are adenine (A), thymine (T), guanine (G) and cytosine (C). Cytosine has a hexagonal shape and is made up of four carbon atoms, three nitrogen atoms, two hydrogen atoms and one oxygen atom. Carbon has an atomic number of six with a nucleus made up four protons and two neutrons that imply the presence of four electrons spinning in its orbit. The diameter of a single atom of carbon is in order of magnitude of $10^{-10}$ cm and its nucleus $10^{-15}$. At greater magnification we enter the zone of quantum mechanics a zone that has always been unimaginable to me. But those who truly understand this mysterious micro-universe claim it to be inhabited by quarks, leptons and bosons. It is reassuring that nuclear physicist believe that space can't be indefinitely divided, and an ultimate horizon of "granularity" is reached at 10 ! In summary, the universe is neither infinitely large nor infinitely small but curiously by chance or design, we stand at the mid-point of this cosmic Uroboros in terms of orders of magnitude based on the centimeter as the unit of measurement. (Uroboros is a mystical snake or dragon that completes a circle by bighting its own tail). Isn't it hubristic to proclaim an anthropocentric concept of the universe with mankind the fulcrum between $10^{30}$ and $10^{-30}$ ? Might this then be interpreted as powerful argument in favor of a creator and our species being the "chosen"? I sense that in asking this question I'm guilty of the logical solecism of circular reasoning (syllogism) or simply restating the "Goldilocks fallacy". This is akin to a fairy-tale heroine who enters the house of the Three Bears and declares the possessions of Baby Bear to be 'just right', as compared to those of Father Bear and Mother Bear, denoting or referring to the most desirable or advantageous part of a range of values or conditions (typically the centre): the planet is in the middle of what astronomers call the **Goldilocks zone**: a place that's not too hot and not too cold.

# Chapter 2

## Was the Spider Created or Did it Evolve?

*All things bright and beautiful,*
*All creatures great and small,*
*All things wise and wonderful:*
*The Lord God made them all.*
HYMNS FOR LITTLE CHILDREN;
CECIL ALEXANDER 1848

ONE OF MY EARLIEST memories was singing this hymn at morning assembly in my infants' school in a small town near Birmingham in about 1943/44. My father sent us there to escape the blitz in London. The hymn had a very catchy melody that I can remember to this day. It was written by Cecil Alexander in 1848 about 10 years before the publication of Charles Darwin's "On the Origin of the Species", at the very time that Darwin was struggling to come to terms between the received wisdom about the creation and his new theory of evolution. Sorry Cecil but I think you lost

## Why Am I a Jew?

the argument. I resent the brain washing that generations of very young and impressionable young people who were taught to believe that the opening passages of Genesis, the first book of the Pentateuch, also known as the five books of Moses, had to be taken at face value. I don't even believe that Moses wrote the five books or took dictation from the Lord God neither do I believe that our world and its denizens, were created in seven days by the King of the Universe. I'm by no means the first to make this bold suggestion, Baruch Spinoza got there first.[1] In that one sentence, I have been guilty of three heresies according to the teachings of orthodox Judaism. This doesn't fill be with foreboding because, a) I can't believe I would be struck down by a God who is sufficiently vain as to be bothered that one of several billion earthlings don't believe he has the capacity to dictate his best work to a mere man, b) Jews, even at the most fundamentalist right wing persuasion, don't issue *fatwas* and c) we very rarely excommunicate each other with the notable exception of Baruch Spinoza, but that was over 350 years ago. The nearest we've come to in the UK, was when Rabbi Louis Jacobs published his book, *We have reason to believe*, in 1957.[2] In this he simply questioned whether the Torah was inspired by God rather than by word of mouth to Moses.

I love the Bible stories and frequently re-read them during the boring sessions of Rosh Hashanah (Jewish New Year) and Yom Kippur (Day of Atonement). The psalms of David, the Book of Ruth, the prophesies of Ezekiel and the Song of Songs, contain beautiful poetry and prose. Yet I cannot accept as truth, the creation myth.

What really annoys me though is the smugness of "creationists" and their belief that acceptance of these childish concepts of the creation somehow makes them better people and more "God fearing". Fearing God in my book, is not a virtue. Behaving yourself because of fear of divine retribution suggests a lower level of ethical development than behaving yourself out of love for your fellow man.

1. Nadler, *A book forged in Hell*, 13–15
2. Freedman, *Reason to believe, The Louis Jacobs affair,*

## Was the Spider Created or Did it Evolve?

I also suggest that "creationism" is a barren way of thinking and a pitiable way of truly appreciating the wonders and beauty of the living world.

So, if my little red spider wasn't created then how did it evolve?

> *As many more individuals of each species are born than can possibly survive; and as, consequently, there is a frequently recurring struggle for existence, it follows that any being, if it vary however slightly in any manner profitable to itself, under the complex and sometimes varying conditions of life, will have a better chance of surviving, and thus be naturally selected. From the strong principle of inheritance, any selected variety will tend to propagate its new and modified form.*

The passage above from Darwin's "On the origin of species" (1859) beautifully, and with a remarkable economy of words, describes the hypothesis that launched a scientific revolution.

Evolutionary theory as described in Darwin's own words is elegant and with great explanatory power. It accounts for the finding of fossils of primitive life forms in the strata of cliff faces on the Dorset coast as well as accounting for the beak shapes of finches found on the Galapagos islands. It also accounts for the comparative skeletal anatomy of different species on view at the Hunterian Museum at the Royal College of Surgeons in London. Furthermore, there are the "natural experiments" of the pre-modern agronomists selecting the most promising of the grass species to cultivate wheat and the breeding of quadrupeds to provide bovine species for milk, genus *ovis aries* for wool and canines as hunting dogs. Other examples where we can witness week by week in a very sinister way with a species of corona virus.

We have been living through a pandemic with a rapidly spreading corona virus that has already killed over 130,000 in the UK. Most news bulletins alarm us when they describe "variants" of the virus that might spread faster than the original COVID-19 or that they may be resistant to our panel of rapidly developed vaccines. They then call upon an expert who explain to lay people the principles natural selection.

# Why Am I a Jew?

So, where does my little red spider fit into the greater scheme of things? When I was a little boy, I was taught this comical yet disturbing rhyme.

> *Big fleas have little fleas upon their back to bite'em.*
> *Little fleas have smaller fleas, and so, proceed ad infinitem.*

This is what is called an infinite regression, just like standing between two mirrors in a dressing room. Well, I'm happy to report that this is not the case for my little red spider. Further research disclosed that she is not a spider after all but a mite. Or to be more specific; *Bryobia praetiosa* (the clover mite). Although a distant relative of *Arachnida* it doesn't weave webs to catch tiny flies but lives off clover. So that's one conundrum of mine resolved. Her humble place in the greater scheme of things is to be at the bottom of some species' food chain. One therefore must assume that without the clover mite, a fault would open-up in our local ecological domain with, who knows what, catastrophic consequences.

# Chapter 3

## *Are We Looking for God in the Wrong Place?*

COMPARED WITH THE AGE of the universe and duration of the evolutionary period on planet earth, not to mention the sojourn time of *homo sapiens,* we are vanishingly small in both in time and space. Neither can we begin to objectify the near infinitely smallness of the space/time niche we occupy. A sense of awe is insufficient, and simply to fill space/time with "God" is an infantile concept that might provide a transient sense of comfort for some. If we endow this "God" with the worst human qualities of vanity (constantly needing praise), vengeance and rage (bullying or frightening us into good behavior) or inducement (promises of reward for obeying man-made laws), then this is not a superhuman worthy of respect but simply man making God in his own image. Again, I find myself rediscovering Spinoza, as exemplified in this first Treatise, *The Ethics.*[1]

I'm not proposing an atheist doctrine, I'm simply suggesting that we are looking for "God" in the wrong places. I believe that

---

1. Scruton, *The Ethics, Prop LX*111, 98–99

"God" is accessible by exploring the near infinitely small spaces within ourselves. These spaces are becoming more and accessible through the ingenuity of *homo sapiens* with the inventions that allow us to explore inner space, where the answers to the length and quality of life exist, rather than outer space where distance is measured in light years. This credo teaches us to love our neighbor as ourselves and that virtue is its own reward. This belief system has had a direct impact on my practice as a surgeon who specialized in treating cancer. This can be simply stated as follows:

The sole purpose of the practice of medicine is to improve the length and quality of life. All other outcome measures are surrogate that seldom translate into these primary objectives.

## THE MIRACLE OF LIFE

Each time the cell divides there is the hazard of a somatic mutation in the genome as a random event. Some cells divide every 48 hours. It is therefore a miracle to me that life can be sustained at all and the question "why me?" whenever someone develops cancer should be reversed, and every day of everyone's life we should offer up a prayer to thank "God" that we *didn't* develop cancer in the previous 24 hours. Richard Dawkins in his most readable and mischievous book "The Blind Watchmaker", describes the fidelity of the transcription process beautifully:

> *"DNA's performance as an archival medium is spectacular. In its capacity to preserve a message it far outdoes tablets of stone. Letters carved on gravestones become unreadable in mere hundreds of years. The DNA document is even more impressive, because unlike tablets of stone it is not the same physical structure that lasts and preserves the text. It is repeatedly being copied and recopied as the generations go by, like the Hebrew Scriptures, which were ritually copied by scribes every eighty years to forestall their wearing out."*

Such precision is miraculous. Life in the first place is miraculous and preservation of our species is miraculous. We should therefore give thanks for this gift however brief the candle within our grasp. But who is this "God" to whom we offer our thanks?

## DO YOU BELIEVE IN "GOD"?

There is an old joke about the dyslexic man who asked, "Do you believe in dog?"!

It's sounds funny because you cannot believe in a noun. You can't believe in cabbage; you can't believe in foot, and you can't believe in Apple. (Mind you my faith in Apple has been strengthened thanks to the spellchecker on my desktop.) You can however believe in Communism or Catholicism. The ism at the end of the word indicates an ideology or a shared belief system. So, the question "Do you believe in 'God'?" is as absurd as "Do you believe in dog?". In this context, the word "God" is used not as an object but as a concept, a belief system or an ism. Yet most lay folk or clergy look upon "God" as "The God" or if they belong to a polytheist faith, "a God". *The* "God" for monotheists and *a* "god" for polytheists. "The God" is visualized in so many ways by different people that I find it impossible to answer the question, "Do you believe in 'God'?" I've literally no idea what the questioner has in mind. I suspect that most people cannot help themselves but to see images, imprinted on their brain, by great works of religious art from the time of the renaissance. Jews and Christian alike will find themselves subconsciously praying to a wise and kindly old man in the sky. The irony here of course is that Jews are not allowed to make images of the almighty. Whenever I think about "God" I see Michelangelo's "Creation of Adam" from the Sistine Chapel, in my mind's eye. Furthermore, I have been taught to see the shape of the human brain and cerebellum in the capsule holding the image of "God" and his heavenly companions.

# Why Am I a Jew?

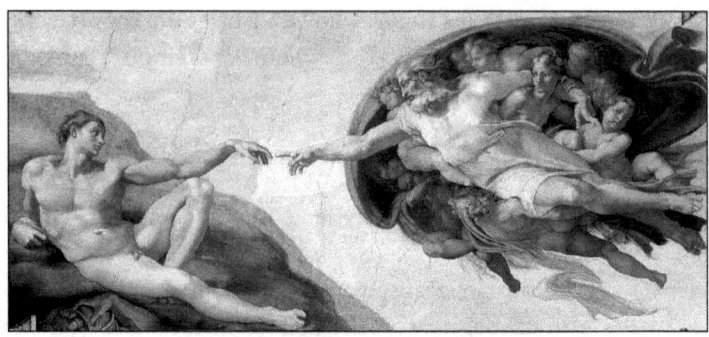

*The Creation of man, Michelangelo, Sistine Chapel roof*

That then reinforces my belief that the direction of causality should be reversed or in other words man's creation of "God". Meanwhile the Jewish teachings hold very clear ideas about some of the attributes of "God" described in Exodus 34:6–7

> *Merciful God, powerful God, compassionate and gracious, slow to anger, and abundant in kindness and truth. Preserver of kindness for thousands of generations, forgiver of iniquity, willful sin and error, and Who cleanses.*

In other words, describing the very best qualities we would like to see in ourselves and our loved ones. Once again, I acknowledge that Spinoza arrived at this insight in the mid 17thC. This then leads us to the perennial question, " . . . if so, who is responsible for all the bad stuff like, and if you'll forgive me for mentioning it; the holocaust?" The two answers from the *faithful* are both unsatisfactory. It's the fault of the devil or it's the will of "God" working in mysterious ways too complex for our understanding. If the former, then we posit two "Gods" one goodie and one baddie. If the latter, then on behalf of the 6M of my tribe, you are not my kind of "God". The late great, Lord Jonathan Sacks, ex chief rabbi of Anglo-Jewry, put it this way in one of his sermons:

> *The question is most acute in relation to the Holocaust itself. Why did G-d not stop the slaughter? To put the dilemma in its sharpest form: Either G-d could not have prevented Auschwitz, or He could but chose not to. If He*

## Are We Looking for God in the Wrong Place?

*could not, how then can He be all-powerful? If He could but did not, how can He be all-good?*

He goes on to describe the fact that Jews have always been struggling with that dilemma and ends up by answering this question with another question.

*The question raised by Auschwitz is not "Where was G-d?" but "Where was man? Where was humanity?"*

I am a great fan of Jonathan Sacks and consider him one of the greatest scholars in 21 C Britain and would be reluctant to challenge him on anything linked to moral philosophy, but I must confess that I find his answer lame. A much simpler answer would be that men can behave badly (an intentional understatement) but we need to consider what *determines* men's bad behavior. "God" cannot or will not control man from without, therefore the only answer is that we are looking for "God" in the wrong place.

I would like to try and explain the paradox described above in evolutionary terms, and again I claim no originality for these ideas. At the time when the first hominids roamed the earth approximately 4M years ago, we can assume that they were organized into extended family groups like we see amongst the great apes today. We can also assume that having the first choice for mates and keeping order in the ranks, was the privilege of the alpha male like the silver-back in a gorilla family. As the species *homo sapiens* emerged we can also assume that a similar pecking order was retained. Extended family groups grew in size if adequate supplies of food were available and natural disasters were avoided. Family groups intermarried until they could be considered a clan or tribe, not only because of blood ties but because of shared rituals and belief systems that incorporated the supernatural. The oldest known representation of a being that does not exist in physical form but symbolizes ideas about the supernatural, is the Lion Man. This 40,000-year-old image was sculpted from mammoth ivory that can be found at the British Museum. From that point on, mankind began to develop more and more complex and sophisticated ideas about mysterious other worlds and a pantheon of other gods that were attributed with hunting skills, controlling weather and being responsible for natural disasters.

The tribe was still controlled by the alpha male chosen for his strength, hunting and fighting skills. If his success was attributed to a supernatural being like the Lion Man, it is more than likely that a wise man emerged from the clan who claimed he could influence this little god for the benefit of the clan. He would have been the first shaman. If the hunting was good, then the shaman and alpha male remained in power. As the tribe leader grew old and weak, he would be challenged in mortal combat by the toughest and most ambitious of the younger males. In contrast the shaman could retain his magic powers as he grew older and thus increase his influence. After a good hunting season, the men might feel like increasing the size of their hunting ground whilst collecting an increasing the number of nubile young women at their disposal. They would then raid the neighboring clans so that the family grew in size and influence. This was not a stable system as there must have been a point when the tribe began to splinter into warring factions and descended into chaos with violence, murder, rape and theft.

Fast forward now from the era of hunter gatherers to the period of the early agronomists and the domestication of wild stock. Then, say about 10,000 years ago, a great clan leader, let's call him Abraham, comes along who is inspired with a great idea. He decides to bring some control and discipline to his unruly tribe. He conceives a great and immortal leader up in the sky with greater powers than any leader in the past. This leader of leaders would be the first God of the monotheistic faiths. This supernatural leader would control the weather and natural disasters and if we behaved. *He* ('twas always thus) would make their flocks fertile and the corn to grow as high as a mastodon's eye. When things went well it was thanks to the beneficent God and if things went badly, it was the fault of members of the tribe, known or unknown, behaving badly. As bad behavior was the norm at that time, most members of the tribe felt guilty when the crops failed or when their flock of goats fell over a cliff. So, at last, after several million years of evolution,

## Are We Looking for God in the Wrong Place?

the first code of conduct began to emerge that ultimately became engraved in tablets of stone by another great leader, Moses. I hope readers don't think I'm being facetious, but those last paragraphs were written with great affection and a sense of awe. *Yes*, it was a good thing when Abraham was inspired by "God", as it was the beginning of an ethical code that defined good behavior. I also believe that at every step of the way, these developments had evolutionary advantages that allowed certain tribes to grow and others to wither. I also believe that in the fullness of time, those members of the successful clan who had inherited a set of genes that in some way encouraged good behavior, became hard wired to see that virtue carried its own reward.

Most animal species demonstrate "moral behavior" that contributes to the common good of the hive or the herd. The argument, however, is whether this is learnt as a way of self-preservation or inherited. How much of this is linked to empathy or altruism is difficult to deduce. Shermer argues that the following qualities are shared by the great apes as well as *homo sapiens*.[2]

> " . . . *attachment and bonding, cooperation and mutual aid, sympathy and empathy, direct and indirect reciprocity, altruism and reciprocal altruism, conflict resolution and peace-making, deception and deception detection, community concern and caring about what others think about you, and awareness of and response to the social rules of the group.*"

To claim that these are learnt skills that are passed on from one generation to another, is akin to Lamarck's theory of evolution through a mechanism for the inheritance of acquired characteristics. I find that implausible. Thomas Huxley, "Darwin's bulldog", pre-empted this debate in his famous lecture at Oxford University in 1893, "Evolution and ethics". He postulated that religion emerged after morality and built upon morality by expanding the social scrutiny of individual behavior to include supernatural agents. By including ever watchful ancestors, spirits and gods in

---

2. Shermer, *The Science of Good and Evil.* 120–121

the social realm, humans discovered an effective strategy for restraining selfishness and building more cooperative groups. The adaptive value of religion would have enhanced group survival. Effectively he was arguing in favor of social evolution as against the ugly bastard child of evolutionary theory, "eugenics".

How social evolution can be "hardwired" into the human genome is way beyond my capacity to describe or even to understand. That is not the point. If we look at the very big picture, we can note that "Evil Empires" collapse as much by implosion as by conquest. That applies to the Babylonian Empire, The Roman Empire, The Ottoman Empire, The Third Reich, The Soviet Empire, and some of the unsavory aspects of the British Empire. Yet over the period spanning nearly 3,000 years, the three Abrahamic faiths, Judaism, Christianity and Islam, have survived. We have recently witnessed the collapse of the so called "Islamic State", that is neither Islamic nor a State, but can only be described as a death cult; only to be replaced by the Taliban in Afghanistan.

At a personal level, we experience a warm glow when we do a good deed, we witness great acts of courage at times of natural disasters, house fires and attacks by terrorists and we recognize altruism amongst members of our society who do essential work for very low pay. Here I'm thinking about the professionalism of nurses, teachers, paramedics, firemen and refuse collectors. Most people reach for a virtuous life and the exceptions we describe as psychopaths or sociopaths. In other words, we brand those rare people who misbehave by nature, as pathological exceptions to the rule. It could be argued that what was started by Abraham with his vision of the Devine has now been overtaken by the works of a raft of philosophers writing from the time of the Enlightenment to the present day who would argue that a belief in "God" is no longer needed as we have now evolved into grown up, rational and ethical beings. This is not hubristic, but a good example of philosophical discourse. As Sir Isaac Newton put it, "If I have seen further, it is by standing on the shoulders of giants".

*Are We Looking for God in the Wrong Place?*

For religious leaders to claim that there is nothing new to learn in moral philosophy as it is all codified in their scriptures, must rank as the ultimate expression of bigotry.

# Chapter 4

## *Development of Ethical Code beyond a Belief in the Supernatural*

AMONG THE PHILOSOPHERS WHO have influenced my thinking I number Maimonides, Michel de Montaigne, Sir Thomas Browne of Norwich, Baruch Spinoza, Voltaire, Immanuel Kant,
 Sir Karl Popper, Chief Rabbi Lord Jakobovits ,, Chief Rabbi Lord Sacks,, Professor Richard Dawkins, Professor Roger Scruton and the late Christopher Hitchens. I wish to be scrupulously honest about the depth of my knowledge and the extent of my reading of the original texts of these authors. I consider myself a dilettante scholar of philosophy yet in some respect I have the advantage of having to put into practice the teachings of these great thinkers in my efforts to save lives. I've read some of the original writings of Rabbi Moishe ben Maimon (Maimonides 1135–1204) in translation of course, including "Guide to the perplexed". He was a man of many parts and worked himself to death as a great Rabbi, great thinker, jurist and a full-time doctor. What I take forward from his work is the idea that a religious and moral life can be good for your health and well-being. (I will return to this later) He is

# Development of Ethical Code beyond a Belief in the Supernatural

most famous for his 13 principles of faith. On re-reading them it's worth noting the first three principles that seem to resonate with the teachings of Spinoza (*vide infra*)

| | |
|---|---|
| Principle 1 | I believe by complete faith that the Creator, blessed be His name, is the Creator and Guide for all created beings. He alone made, makes, and will make all that is created. |
| Principle 2 | I believe by complete faith that the Creator, blessed be His name, is a Unity, and there is no union in any way like Him. He alone is our God, who was, who is, and who is to be. |
| Principle 3 | I believe by complete faith that the Creator, blessed be His name, is not a body, is not affected by physical matter, and nothing whatsoever can compare to Him [or be compared with Him]. |

I read Michel de Montaigne's (1533–1592) essays from cover to cover and learnt from his writings that a life of reflection, thinking through moral dilemmas and rationalizing empirical observations, helps creativity and is good for peace of mind. Of course, he was an aristocrat who didn't have to work for a living, I had to wait for retirement to enjoy the leisure of reflection and creativity. Montaigne invented the mode of writing we now describe by the word *essay* derives from the French infinitive *essayer*, "to try" or "to attempt". In other words, to put on trial. Having just written that I was minded taking another look at Montaigne's essays after nearly 20 years of neglect. I'm using the Penguin Classics edition with a brilliant translation by J. M. Cohen.[1] I'd forgotten what a delight it was to read, as if the author was speaking directly to you over the passage of more than four centuries. His charm lies in the use of the first person throughout and the avoidance of the passive tense. He is even self-deprecating for his apparent egotism and tongue in cheek, claims that no one else has the expertise to compete with him in writing about himself. Here is a passage where he warns the reader against accepting received wisdom.

> The tutor should make his pupil sift everything and take nothing into his head on simple authority or trust.

1. Montaigne M, *Essays*

# Why Am I a Jew?

> *Aristotle's principles must no more be principles with him than those of the Stoics or the Epicureans. Let their various opinions be put before him; he will choose between them if he can, if not he will remain in doubt. Only fools are certain and immovable.*

In other words, faith is no virtue, but uncertainty is! Then later, in a chapter headed Repentance he writes:

> *There is indeed a certain sense of gratification when we do a good deed that gives us inward satisfaction, and a generous pride that accompanies a good conscience . . . .*
>
> *These testimonies of a good conscience are pleasant; and such natural pleasure is very beneficial to us; it is the only payment that can never fail.*

Yet again, a great thinker argues that virtue carries its own reward. What a lovely man he must have been.

Sir Thomas Browne (1605–1682) was an Englishman, an essayist like Montaigne but also earnt a living as a physician and was appointed to the court of King Charles II. I own a collection of all his works and love the volume entitled "Vulgar errors".[2] Browne used the simple technique of rational thinking and testing the received wisdom by the expedient of observation. He was the first to make the observation that men and women have the same number of ribs *ergo*, Eve couldn't have been created from one of Adam's ribs. I'm also indebted to him for disproving the belief that you can tell that a Jew is nearby from his characteristic stink.[3] His essay starts like this:

> *"That Jews stink, that in their race is an evil savor, is a received opinion we know not how to admit."*

He then goes on for three or four closely argued pages describing the history of the Jews, the laws of their diet and their laws of hygiene and suggests, that if anything we should expect that Jews smell sweeter than Christians. He concludes that this must be the case because of a simple empirical observation.

2. Browne, T, *The Works of Sir Thomas Browne, ReligioMedici*, 214–216
3. Browne, T, *The Works of Sir Thomas Browne, Vulgar Errors*, 413–421

## Development of Ethical Code beyond a Belief in the Supernatural

> *"Lastly, experience will convict it; for this offensive odor is no way discoverable in their synagogues where many are and by reason of their number could not be concealed"*

Note the expression "received opinion".

From that alone we know he must be one of the pioneers of the age of enlightenment.

Coming back to Baruch Spinoza (1632–77); the excommunicated Jew from Amsterdam.

Well, he deserves two chapters on his own later in this book, but I confess that Sir Richard Scruton's writings assisted me in understanding Spinoza's logic. [4]

Francoise-Marie Arouet (1694–1778) also known as Voltaire, is great fun and a ready source of aphorisms, almost as good as Oscar Wide. He is well known for his hostility to Christianity and for that matter, Judaism, and is clearly in the camp of latter day atheists such as Christopher Hitchens and Richard Dawkins. However, he has something useful to say about fanaticism that I will return to in the section below concerning the ugly side of religious beliefs.

As far as Hitchens and Dawkins our concerned, I think I've read pretty much all they've written. At one point in my life, I claimed I was a Dawkins kind of Jew but as you will see I've shifted my position to claim that I am a Spinoza kind of Jew.

The others in my list of philosophers that have influenced my thinking; Immanuel Kant, Sir Karl Popper (who befriended me), Chief Rabbi Lord Jakobovits and Chief Rabbi Lord Sacks (both of whom officiated at my younger daughter's wedding). They will make their presence felt in the later section of this dissertation in relation to my views on how to conduct our lives today, using the bedrock of the Bible. For now, I want to express my thoughts on the Good, the Bad and the Ugly of the most influential monotheistic religions over the last 3,000 years.

---

4. Scruton R, *Spinoza, A very short introduction*

# Chapter 5

## *The Good, the Bad and the Ugly of Monotheistic Religions*

LET'S REVERSE THE ORDER and start with the ugly. "Ugly" doesn't do justice to the strength of my feelings when I consider what the monotheistic religions have shown themselves capable of.

For the last three millennia until the present day, unbelievable atrocities have been committed in the name of the one "true god". I use the word unbelievable because even if one side of my brain knows it's true the other side of my brain says, "surely mankind can't be that evil, vile (an anagram of evil), debauched, depraved, malicious, cruel, hateful, maleficent and every other word for describing the worst possible behavior imaginable". This behavior even goes beyond the international laws concerning genocide and ethnic cleansing. There are no words that I can find to describe my revulsion at the act of burning someone alive for heresy in medieval times or decapitating them for not swearing allegiance to the prophet in the cesspit of what was known as "Islamic State". I shudder now to think how the Afghan women might be treated in the near future.

# The Good, the Bad and the Ugly of Monotheistic Religions

The story of wholesale massacre starts in the Old Testament that provides many distasteful examples that provide little credit for the reputation of the ancient Israelites. Israel seemed to be constantly at war with the Philistines in the battles to occupy the "Promised Land". Here is one example of what might be considered a minor skirmish described in the book of Samuel c1,000 BCE.

> 18:25 *And Saul said, Thus, shall ye say to David, the king desireth not any dowry, but an hundred foreskins of the Philistines, to be avenged of the king's enemies. But Saul thought to make David fall by the hand of the Philistines.*

> 18:26 *And when his servants told David these words, it pleased David well to be the king's son in law: and the days were not expired.*

> 18:27 *Wherefore David arose and went, he and his men, and slew of the Philistines two hundred men; and David brought their foreskins, and they gave them in full tale to the king, that he might be the king's son in law. And Saul gave him Michal his daughter to wife.*

Of course, since the Israelites were driven out of their land by the Romans at the fall of the second Temple in 70 CE, they have not had their own army to wage another holy war until, in theory, 1948. The nascent State of Israel had to fight for its very existence then and at intervals ever since. They have been accused of disproportionate aggression after the provocation by Hamas lobbing 7,000 rockets over the border, but these aren't "holy wars" but merely responding to an existential threat. Nevertheless, when I listen to rhetoric of some spokesmen from the settlers' movement, I believe they would be capable of mounting a "Holy war" to regain control of the whole of the lands of Judea and Samaria that constituted the land of Israel in Biblical times.

The biggest problem the Jews have faced over the last 2,000 years have been thanks to the followers of Jesus of Nazareth. There is a prayer that we say at the most solemn part of the service in the synagogue on Yom Kippur known as *Unesanneh Tokef* (הנתנו תקף) *"Let us speak of the awesomeness "*. It was composed by an

## Why Am I a Jew?

11th-century sage named Rabbi Amnon of Mainz in Germany. He was a close friend and confidant of the Archbishop of Mainz. Rabbi Amnon was pressured to convert to Catholicism. As a delaying tactic, he requested three days to consider the offer; immediately he regretted intensely giving even the pretense that he could possibly accept conversion to another religion. After spending the three days in prayer, he refused to come to the archbishop as promised, and, when he was forcibly brought to the archbishop's palace, he begged that his tongue be cut out to atone for his sin. Instead, the archbishop ordered his hands and legs amputated — limb by limb — as punishment for not obeying his word to return after three days and for refusing to convert. At each amputation, Rabbi Amnon was again given the opportunity to convert, which he refused. He was sent home, with his severed extremities, on his litter. As he lay dying, he composed the prayer that celebrated the awesomeness of God.

This is a legend and may not be true but consider the abomination of the Spanish and Portuguese inquisition in the late 15 and early 16 C where torture, mutilation and the pyre were rife for heretics and Jews who refused to convert. Turning the story on its head, if the Amnon of Mainz had been a catholic, he would have been canonized for his faith and an addressee for intersessional prayer for those suffering from say, gangrene. These one on one crimes by the agents of the faith have an immediacy we can easily grasp, but when it comes to holy wars between different interpretations of Christianity, the Crusades with Christians massacring Jews *en route* to Jerusalem to set about massacring Muslims, the mass murders, the pogroms and ethnic cleaning, you can multiply this by the 10s of thousands. Even as I write human rights organizations have reported horrific crimes against the Rohingya (Muslims) living in Myanmar where the state religion is Theravada Buddhism. Their homes and villages have been burned down and destroyed, children were taken away and killed, women violently raped, civilians brutally beaten before being burned. As a result, nearly 1M are living in vile conditions at the border with Bangladesh. Whilst Boko Haram, a Sunni Muslim group in Nigeria, terrorizes the Christians and abducts hundreds of girls into forced marriages. At the same time Shiite extremists, like Hamas, take pleasure in throwing homosexuals off the roof in Gaza.

You will of course be saying to yourself what about the evil ideologies of fascism, Stalinism and Maoism? To which I will reply that I am not talking about Fascism, Stalinism and Maoism, I'm talking about religion that is meant to ensure our virtuous behavior. The fact that these other ideologies are just as bad is no comfort to me. There must be something about religions with millions of devotees that is rotten at the core. The "great" monotheistic faiths were intended to save us from sin yet taking their broad history over the last three millennia, I think we might be better off with a bit more sin! A touch of larceny, philandering, dishonesty and a murder or two, would be a damn sight better than the wholescale mayhem inflicted on the world in the name of the "one true god".

To an extent, religion played its part in the holocaust as endemic antisemitism in Germany and Austria provided a useful culture medium for Nazism to flourish. Furthermore, Stalin blamed the "cosmopolitan capitalists" (code words for the Jews) to account for the bankruptcy of the USSR.

Let me tell you a story about a visit to Germany about 20 years ago. I was a member of the faculty of a conference on biostatistics at Freiberg University. Freiberg is a very pretty city with a central square that sports a magnificent cathedral. During a break in the afternoon, we were taken on a tour of the cathedral with a young lady who spoke perfect English, as a guide. I remember that it was a very sunny day, and we were all dappled in bright colors from the sun blazing through the stained-glass windows. Our guide then described the narratives illustrated by these windows that were constructed not just to beautify the house of prayer, but to act like a strip cartoon or a graphic novel for the benefit of the illiterate 13th C congregation. The story the windows told was nothing other than the "blood libel". In each meticulously created work of art with a translucent mosaic of color, we see sinister Jews in their characteristic pointed hats as they go about abducting and murdering a blond Christian child, draining his blood and using it to make the matzo bread for the Passover. It was the guide herself, not one of the shocked academics in the group, who pointed out how deeply engrained antisemitism was in the German psyche. I was glad to leave the cathedral and breath some fresh air free from the incense that stank of ritualized hatred. Our guide then took as to the opposite side of the square facing the cathedral and drew our attention to a beautiful modern and gracious three-story building and it explained it was their new synagogue. Without thinking I burst out, "I had no idea that Jews had returned to Freiberg". To which she replied, "They haven't but we want them to return, and this is the symbol of our good will and contrition for our past".

I can sense that some of my co-religionists and members of other faiths getting fidgety, wanting to interrupt my rant. I can almost hear their words; "That was then, this is now, the bad guys weren't true Jews, Christians, Muslims ( . . . enter other faiths as you see fit), they have given our religion a bad reputation." I can even hear the late great, Jonathan Sacks speaking out in support of all the other faiths, "Where was man? Where was humanity?"

I'm tired of this constant apologia from the faith communities following on from each act of barbarity of man on fellow man. You can't blame God and you can't blame religion. God is responsible for all the good stuff and all religions preach peace and kindness. If it's all man's fault, how can we believe that man was created in God's image? Of course, "God" didn't say man was created in his image, whoever wrote that section in the Bible said that. In writing those words one suspects that the author had in mind only the very best of mankind's attributes. The worst attributes of man would be atavistic, in other words those of the animal kingdom. That doesn't make sense either, because animal on fellow animal attack is nothing like the worst crimes of man on fellow man. A pack of lions doesn't hunt down other packs of lions. A pack of lions, hunts down zebras, not because they are black and white (also known as "zebra phobia") no, lions hunt zebras for lunch as part of an ecological chain.

The other paradox is that we've just established the evolutionary advantage of altruism and that virtue of virtue. Yet in every episode of butchery in the name of "god" we witness hatred replacing the command and the instinct to love our neighbor. The only explanation must be the toxic effects of an ideology, and here I include religious faith, that is capable of being used a catalyst to foment crowd insanity. If we can track down that source of the "Devil's spark", we might be halfway to its cure.

I will attempt to do this using my training in the scientific method, root cause analysis and logic. The example I will focus on might be considered as a "natural experiment".

On Friday the 25th of November 2017, a group of terrorists, linked to Sunni Muslim organizations active in the Sinai Peninsula, murdered more than 300 worshipers in a mosque associated with the Sufi branch of the Sunni interpretation of Islam. Having bombed the mosque at the height of the Friday prayers they then set about mowing down men, women and children with machine guns mounted on trucks outside, as the survivors tried to escape.

Tut, tut, this is truly awful behavior by any standard. What's more I can't help but see the tragic irony in that this outrage was acted out in the neighborhood of mount Sinai, where Moses is said to have scratched the words of God on tablets of stone; "THOU SHALT NOT KILL"!

I will try and analyze this event by answering the following questions:

- What is the difference between Sufi and orthodox interpretations of Sunni Islam?
- Do these differences represent an existential threat to Islam?
- If not, then what motivated the attack?
- If we can answer that question, then who is responsible for the interpretations of the Koran or the Hadith that justified this mass murder?
- If we can answer that then by what means were the pack of murderers sufficiently inflamed to create this atrocity? [1]

- If we can answer that question, we can hand over the perpetrators to the agencies of the secular law and hand over the preachers of hate to the appropriate religious authorities.
- Finally, if the religious authorities won't act then the secular authorities must intervene.

Using root cause analysis let's see how many of these questions I can answer.

Firstly, what is the difference between Sufi and orthodox interpretations of Sunni Islam?

Apart from all the Islamic scholars reading this book, like you, I must have a quick look at Wikipedia. For a start, we can simply check out the six principal articles of faith, essential for salvation, upon which the Sunni branch of Islam stands. These are:

- Belief in the One God
- Belief in the existence of angels
- Belief in the existence of prophets
- Belief in God's revelations, including the Torah (revealed to Moses), the Psalms (revealed to David), the Gospel (revealed to Jesus), and the Quran (revealed to Muhammad)
- Belief in the Day of Judgment
- Belief in God's predestination

Let me then see what if anything in the Sufi interpretation of Sunni Islam challenges even one of these principles of faith. From the little I know, Sufism takes a mystical approach to Islam and its followers, worship at shrines and pray for the intercession of saints, yet it is reported that the Imam officiating at the time of the atrocity opened prayers with the words, "In the name of God, the most merciful and compassionate." I confess to nothing other than a shallow understanding of Islam, neither am I up to the effort of embarking on another long avenue of scholarship in my advanced

## The Good, the Bad and the Ugly of Monotheistic Religions

years, so I will take on trust that the extracts from an essay by Dr Javad Nurbakhsh provide a sense of how Sufi's conduct their life.[1]

> *In Sufi practice, quietism and seclusion—sitting in isolation, occupying oneself day and night in devotions—are condemned. All masters of the Path have had active professional lives, never freeloading off society. All Sufis are enjoined to have jobs, work productively in society, earn wages and support their families. Above all, they must serve others. . . . . . . One's intention is focused on God alone, for in being a lover of God, one seeks nothing of God's creatures in one's practice of loving Him.*

Is there anything in this that could be interpreted as an existential threat to Islam? Certainly, no suggestion I could find, although the online Isis magazine, al-Nabaa, declared, "Our primary focus lies in the war against polytheism and apostasy, and of those Sufism, sorcery and divination". Hardly adequate conditions to motivate mass murder that included 27 children.

Who is responsible for the interpretations of the Koran or the Hadith that justified this mass murder? I've no idea and no way of finding out. That is a job for agents in the field.

If we can't answer that for the time being, then at least can try to understand by what means were this pack of murderers sufficiently inflamed to create this atrocity? I can at least begin to understand the methods used by the instigators of such repulsive and merciless behavior because we have been here before in living memory. Let me start by quoting from Voltaire's description of Fanaticism from his philosophical dictionary.

> *"Once fanaticism has cankered a brain, the disease is almost incurable. How can you answer a man who tells you that he would rather obey God than men, and who therefore sure deserve heaven in cutting your throat? Religion far from being a beneficial food in such cases, turns into poison in effected brains. There is no other remedy for this epidemic illness than the spirit of free thought . . . . . . "*

---

1. Nurbakhsh, J, *Discourses on the Sufi path.*

## Why Am I a Jew?

It is interesting that Voltaire uses the words cancer and poison of the brain as an epidemic illness. He offers little in the way of public health measures that might prevent such epidemics. We should therefore look at the history of cholera and the observations of Doctor John Snow, who controlled an epidemic in Soho, central London, by simply removing the handle of the Broad Street pump in 1854. How did Hitler and his henchman, Joseph Goebbels, transmute the sophisticated and cultured citizens of Germany, into the slavering, mindless Rottweilers of the Nazi SS divisions? Let's see how far the cholera analogy will take us.

In the mid 19thC, the population of London's Soho were dirt poor, starving and living in rat infested hovels. The government of the day was corrupt and indifferent to their problems. The only source of water for washing, cooking and drinking was the cholera infested contents from a cistern that was fractured so that the water from the Thames was contaminated by the sewage from the neighborhood.

Germany during the period of the Weimar Republic, in the mid 1920s was in a serious financial crisis because of the punitive reparations agreed at the Versailles peace conference. The population of Berlin were dirt poor, starving and living in rat infested hovels. The government of the day was corrupt and indifferent to their problems. Unemployment was at a peak and inflation astronomical. There only hope for these desperate folk, appeared to be the nascent Nazi party who promised a bright future with vacations in the fresh Alpine air and lakes, for everyone. Sadly, for the Germans and for the rest of the world, the ideology of Herr Hitler although sounding bracing at the time, was infested with something worse than cholera; bacillus National Socialism (Nazism).

During the COVID-19 pandemic I have experienced more frequent antisemitism online, as have my Jewish colleagues. This is no surprise. The scapegoating of Jews during infectious disease outbreaks and the stereotyping of Jews as vectors of disease has a long, ingrained history, going back to at least the 14th century when Jews were blamed for the Black Death. Adolf Hitler famously resurrected this theme when he wrote: "I feel I am like Robert

Koch in politics. He discovered the bacillus and thereby ushered medical science onto new paths. I discovered the Jew as the bacillus and fermenting agent of all social decomposition." Note that Hitler described the Jews as the vector of disease whereas in truth the germ that has killed millions in the Holocaust was the virus of anti-Semitism. This virus was highly infectious because of the culture medium of the times and entered the population in three steps, blaming others for their problems, dehumanizing these "others" and mass propaganda that led to mass hysteria.

In sociology and psychology, mass hysteria (also known as collective hysteria, group hysteria, or collective obsessional behavior) is a phenomenon that transmits collective illusions of threats, whether real or imaginary, through a population in society as a result of rumors and fear. Sir Simon Wesley and colleagues summed it up like this.

> "Mass hysteria is a sociogenic illness mirrors prominent social concerns, changing in relation to context and circumstance (including hysteria from the topic at hands). Prior to the 1900, reports are dominated by episodes of motor symptom's typified by psychological agitation incubated in an environment of pre-existing tension."

This was clearly the intention of Hitler's Nuremberg Rallies orchestrated by Joseph Goebbels. Brunhilde Pomsel was one of Goebbels' private secretaries who lived through two world wars and died on holocaust Memorial Day in 2016 at the age of 106. She suffered no remorse and claimed that she was naïve, ignorant and disinterested in politics. She probably represented a large percent of the German population at that time who chose not to know what was going on during the Nazi era.

The "others" in the Nazi propaganda who could be blamed for the privations of the German people were the Jews, they were dehumanized in the rhetoric of Hitler and Goebbels and the films produced by Goebbels's propaganda industry, as vermin and rats. In addition, Eugene Fischer, Hitler's professor of eugenics in Berlin, published papers and delivered lectures, where the Jews were described as sub-human based on pseudo-scientific morphometrics. With that, the scene was set for the Holocaust.

George Orwell wrote a brilliant and terrifying satire on this in his book 1984 (published in 1948) where he describes the daily "two minute's hate" that all the staff of "The Ministry of Truth" had to attend.

> *The next moment a hideous, grinding speech, as of some monstrous machine running without oil, burst from the big telescreen at the end of the room. It was a noise that set one's teeth on edge and bristled the hair at the back of one's neck. The Hate had started. As usual, the face of Emmanuel Goldstein, the Enemy of the People, had flashed on to the screen. In its second minute the Hate rose to a frenzy. People were leaping up and down in their places and shouting at the tops of their voices in an effort to drown the maddening bleating voice that came from the screen. The little sandy-haired woman had turned bright pink, and her mouth was opening and shutting like that of a landed fish. Even O'Brien's heavy face was flushed. He was sitting very straight in his chair, his powerful chest swelling and quivering as though he were standing up to the assault of a wave. The dark-haired girl behind Winston had begun crying out "Swine! Swine! Swine!" and suddenly she picked up a heavy Newspeak dictionary and flung it at the screen.*

So that is how it's done. I have little doubt that the murderous devotees of some warped interpretation of Islam, guilty of the barbaric attack in Egypt and no doubt affiliated to Islamic State, were subjected to a program of brain washing and more than two minutes a day for the preaching of hatred to "the other", in this case the Sufis. This process is aided and abetted by the social media available on millions of smart phones in circulation in the Middle East and North Africa. It is therefore imperative of the World's leaders of the true peace-loving Islamic faith, a faith that endorses the edict to "Love thy neighbor", to identify those responsible, excommunicate them or issue a fatwa against them.

> *"We believe in God, and the revelation given to us, and to Abraham, Ishmai'l, Isaac, Jacob, and the Tribes, and that*

## The Good, the Bad and the Ugly of Monotheistic Religions

> given to Moses and Jesus, and that given to (all) Prophets form their Lord: We make no difference between one and another of them: And we submit to God." Nobel Qur'an (2:13)

In many western countries, there are civil laws that make the preaching of hate a crime, so these miscreants should also be handed over to secular authorities and face the law of the land. Finally, if the religious authorities of certain countries who covertly endorse this obscene behavior, won't act, then the secular authorities must intervene, and diplomatic overtures have been snubbed; then *we* have *causus belli*. Religious terrorism is a multi-headed hydra so it will be necessary to go for the heart of the beast rather than its extremities. The flaw in this line of argument is in the single word *we*. Who are the global police forces and who are the legions of the righteous who will wage war against these merchants of evil? It takes a vote at the UN to deploy troops to areas of conflict and their rules of engagement are so stringent that more often than not, they simply act as observers. Furthermore, the perpetrators of these crimes against humanity may have a casting vote in the hallowed halls of the UN thus making the institution unfit for purpose. All this was being played out in front of our eyes as we watched the TV news at the time of the Taliban were taking over the government of Afghanistan and promising they would govern according to the laws of Sharia. I take little comfort in that reassurance

## THE BAD

Having dealt with the ugly side of religion that indulges in mass murder and torture, let us raise our sights and just look and the bad side of religion. Of course, religion never set out to endorse bad behavior it merely codified the accepted standards of the times based on the literal interpretation of the scriptures by nomadic tribes wandering in the desert a long time ago. Times have since changed often for the betterment of mankind. Moral philosophy has made progress over the absolutism of the past in the same way that scientific philosophy has contributed to a longer and better quality of life for all. The religious establishment wishes to enjoy the fruit but deny the tree. Here is my list of my most un-favorite things that apply to most of the orthodox interpretations of the monotheistic religions. I'm not saying that these teachings should be proscribed but I don't think they add to the sum of human happiness.

- Belief in Heaven and hell
- Teaching of sexual guilt
- Denial of sexual orientation
- Promotion of celibacy as a virtue
- Anti-abortion and contraception
- Misogyny

The Christian vision of Heaven looks like hell to me. Imagine an eternity in the company of sanctimonious saints, pious priests and miserable monks. I'd rather the company of Voltaire, Modigliani and Donizetti, assuming we could all understand each other. Seriously, teaching the faithful that their reward for good behavior will be in Heaven again implies that virtue is practiced for reward and encourages the poor and miserable to believe that if they suffer in silence then life after death would be a better place than life on earth. This way the powerful clerics at the top of the hierarchy of the church will remain in power and secular powers responsible for the crushing poverty of the underclass can retain the status quo without fear of an insurrection. Karl Marx was right to say that "religion was the opiate of the masses".

Islam's vision of Heaven sounds like a lot of fun, well at least for men. Here is one description I discovered on the internet.

> *Surat number 52 verse 17, "Verily, the pious will be in gardens, and the delight, enjoying in that which their lord has bestowed on them. And their lord saved them from the torment of the blazing fire, eat and drink with happiness because of what you used to do. They would recline on*

> beds, arranged in ranks, and we shall marry them to fair women with wide, lovely eyes."

The precise number of these women with lovely eyes appears to be debatable but it is in the order of 70–100. So again, it is not virtue for virtues sake but virtue for the bribe of paradise. For my personal tastes, that kind of number of wives would be hell! Imagine if they synchronized their menstrual cycle and if all of them suffered premenstrual tension at the same time. Imagine the jealousy and intrigue. *Oy vaiz meer!* (Yiddish for "woe is me"). Of course, anyone can make fun of these beliefs and it's a cheap and disrespectful joke. Visions of heaven in the Quran and the Hadith are written in beautiful poetry by scribes from the 7 to the 9 C CE and my sources tell me that Muslims believe that God dictated the Quran to the Prophet over a 30-year period in the early 7 C. In these years, amongst the nomadic tribes in the deserts of the Middle East, a Paradise of beautiful gardens, fountains, songbirds and beautiful women, would indeed be a rich reward for a good life spent in such austere conditions. I don't want to make fun of this in its original context, but to appropriate this vision as a reward for naïve, dirt poor, ill-educated youths, to sacrifice their lives as suicide bombers, is a profanity to me as it must be to all my Muslim friends.

Hell is something else! It's not just a question of going up or going down after death, it's a vile concept created by some very sick minds in the dark ages. Just look at Hieronymus Bosch's vision of Hell, It is currently in the Doges' Palace in Venice, Italy. It illustrates an eternity of the worst tortures that could be dreamed up by sadistic agents of the tribunal of the holy office of the inquisition. *Dante* Alighieri has a lot to answer for as well, with his epic poem, "Inferno", the first part of the "Divine Comedy". Some comedy. He describes the Seventh Circle of Hell divided into three rings. The Outer Ring houses murderers and others who were violent to other people and property. Here, Dante sees notable historical and mythological figures, sinking into a river of boiling blood and fire. In the Middle Ring, the poet sees suicides who have been turned into trees and bushes which are fed upon by harpies. In the Inner

Ring are blasphemers and sodomites, residing in a desert of burning sand and burning rain falling from the sky. Once again virtue is not its own reward but an insurance against an eternity of fire and brimstone. I think civilization has moved on a bit since the 14 C. We no longer should be terrifying young children with this nightmare visions as punishment for bad behavior. To me it's a form of child abuse.

When it comes to sex, the religious hierarchy really "get their knickers in a twist"! It's as if the fact that sexual intercourse, a necessary activity for the continuation of our species, happens to be pleasurable to such an extent that it must be a sin. Sure, there are those who abuse the gift a sexual pleasure and are guilty of rape, pedophilia, sexual grooming of vulnerable young women, sexual slavery, and sexually aggravated assault. These crimes are dealt with by the police and the judiciary and it's in the individuals enlightened self-interest, to avoid such crimes or else expect a lengthy sojourn in the clink. That immediate threat is probably more effective than the threat of a longer sentence in worse condition after death. Other bad sexual behavior such as sexual harassment of vulnerable young men and women are dealt with by public revulsion when exposed in the media. Such men (it is always men) stand to lose their jobs and become pariahs in polite society. Promiscuity and infidelity share the same opprobrium and carry the risk of STDs. In same way that virtue is its own reward, so does sin carry its own punishment.

Sex between consenting adults is none of the business of the clergy. The same applies with same sex relationships. Sexual orientation is a complex biological and psychological phenomenon and if the result is homosexuality and the relationships are built on love, what business is it of the pious to spread guilt and fear amongst this significant minority that has always existed in society. Once again, I must mention the danger and consequences of promiscuity as equally applied to heterosexuals.

The Catholic church promotes the idea that celibacy as a virtue and this is a pre-requisite for the priesthood. I look upon this as a bad idea for the three reasons. Firstly, there would be a bias amongst those who would apply for ordination. This bias would favor those men who are effectively asexual. It wouldn't require much self-control for asexual men of the cloth and as a result they may severely judge those poor men and women in the confessional who admitted to the sin of extra-marital sexual congress. The second problem I see is for the unfortunate young priest who does indeed retain a normal sexual drive. He will constantly be in a state of guilt as he constantly resists temptation. Furthermore, the inevitable nocturnal emission associated with lurid dreams, will have him running to the confessional himself once a week. Thirdly and of most grave concern, are the priests who are in the habit of giving way to temptation and become guilty of molesting vulnerable young men and women in their congregation. There have been too many such episodes and the Catholic Church have been too willing to cover them up in the past.

The anti-abortion lobby fueled by the faithful is a difficult issue to deal with but if you'll forgive me, I'd like to introduce it with an old joke.

A Catholic priest, a Church of England Vicar and a Rabbi from the United Synagogue, were on a panel discussing the topic of abortion. The chairman of the panel asked the three men their opinions on when life begins. The Catholic Priest insisted it was at the point of conception, the Vicar from the Church of England politely disagreed and thought life began at the point when a fetus can survive outside the uterus. The Rabbi was in no doubt; "Life begins when the children leave home, and the dog dies!".

It is not a laughing matter. Personally, I don't think it is any business of old celibate cardinals to tell unfortunate young women how to deal with an unwanted pregnancy that might have been the consequence of rape. I also object to the rhetoric of the so-called "pro-lifers" who describe abortion as murder and intimidate the clients and the medical staff of the abortion clinic. All I know for sure is that there is too much unhappiness in the world today for young women who are pregnant out of wedlock at one extreme and middle-aged women who simply can't cope with the

7th pregnancy forced upon her because of the strictures against safe contraception.

Finally, misogyny. The founding fathers of the three Abrahamic faiths lived at a time when polygamy was the norm. There might even have been an evolutionary advantage to this arrangement. With many wives, with many children, with little domestic help and no labor-saving devices apart from the odd Nubian slave, women didn't have much leisure to indulge themselves in the Priesthood, involve themselves in the dialectic on the meaning of life and the attributes of the almighty, the composition of the liturgy and the judgement on their fellow man. As Cicero once said *"O tempora o mores!"* (Different times, different manners.) It's shameful that the orthodox religious authorities are amongst the last to accept equal rights for women in the home, at work and at worship.

My son lives in New Jersey, USA and is a member of a rather liberal Hebrew congregation. Two of my grandsons celebrated their Bar Mitzvah there. My wife and I loved the ceremony whilst my other grandchildren from London looked on agog. My daughters were called up to open the Ark and my wife was invited up to read from the Torah (there's a first time for everything). The assistant Rabbi and cantor was a woman with a wonderful voice who accompanied herself on a lute, whilst her partner and their child joined in from the side, this being a same sex marriage. Some of our friends and relatives, all of whom might be liberal in their attitude, might have been surprised. Yet had they have been there they would have noted the total involvement of the community and their love for each other. At the end of the service, we were all called up to the *Bimah* (Platform), four tall men held the corners of a huge prayer shawl over us, and the senior Rabbi blessed us all, men and women alike. The symbolism was self-evident.

# The Good, the Bad and the Ugly of Monotheistic Religions

## THE GOOD

> "The evil that men do lives after them; The good is oft interèd with their bones"
>
> Shakespeare. *Julius Caesar*, Act 2, Scene 3
>
> "All right, but apart from the sanitation, the medicine, education, wine, public order, irrigation, roads, a freshwater system, and public health, what have the Romans ever done for us?"
>
> Monty Python, *Life of Brian*

I hope those two quotations flag up the direction I'm about to take.

If you've read this far you might have started to believe that I was an atheist but as already described the question, "do you believe in God?" is a meaningless formulation of words. If you get to the end of this book, you will be in a good position to judge my answer, but that answer might not apply to your own construct of the nature of God.

I hereby declare that there has been and will always be a role for religion because of the good it can achieve. At this point I depart from the position adopted by two of my heroes, Christopher Hitchens and Richard Dawkins. Their arguments against the existence of the conventional beliefs about "God" are difficult to refute, but then they are liberal, metropolitan sophisticates with intelligence quotients above 130. It is a joke to say that 50% of the population are below average intelligence but it is not a joke to say that more than 50% of the world's population have been denied a liberal education and that is often the case in countries where the ruling class in dominated by the religious hierarchy. The hard-core atheists seem to assume that there will be a golden age in the future when everyone will be cured of "the God delusion". Until that time comes, where do these poor, uneducated, unsophisticated human beings look for hope at times of despair, comfort at times of fear and consolation at the time of bereavement? "Humanism" has yet to offer anything robust enough to replace faith, hope and charity.

Now I come to think about it, "humanism" has so far contributed nothing of value to my life or the lives of my family.

Let me start with a small example of how Christianity saved my sanity (I will devote a whole chapter to the role of Judaism in my life). When I was first appointed Professor of Surgery at University College London, my clinical practice was confined to the old Middlesex hospital. This hospital was built in 1745 and "modernized" in 1928! By the time I started working there in 1999, the conditions were squalid, the wards were overcrowded, and my out-patient clinic was in what used to be the local workhouse that hadn't been redecorated since the days of Charles Dickens. My workload was insufferable, and I started feeling the prodromal symptoms of clinical depression. There was, however, a secret retreat for me and that was the pretty little hospital chapel that had kept its charms for over 200 years. I would often slip into this oasis of tranquility, sit on a pew in a dark corner and feel my muscles relax and a sense of peace envelope me. The combination of quietude, colored light refracted through stained glass windows, the embroidered trappings over the altar and pulpit, and the smell of polished wood was therapeutic. I didn't pray I simply sat there and imagined I was surrounded by the ghosts of patients past who had also sought comfort and spiritual support at a time of existential threat. Houses of congregation and prayer act as retreats from the harshness of reality of the human condition. This should not be mocked.

This then leads me on to the heritage religion left to us in the form of the art, architecture, choral singing and the liturgy of houses of prayer. Constable's painting of Salisbury Cathedral serves two purposes in that it illustrates the beauty of the architecture and reflects the inspiration of the Church of England on England's greatest landscape artist. The Cathedral also inspired Ken Follett to write the book "Pillars of the Earth" that describes the impact on a mediaeval community tasked with building a heavenly version of Jerusalem on England's green and pleasant land. This was at a time when the expectation of life was about 30 years and most of the population lived in squalor. You must share my sense of outrage to learn that scarce resources of labor, materials and gold went towards the building of a house for "God" rather than warm and dry homes for the stonemasons and their families. I recently visited Naples and was struck dumb by the interior of the Cathedral that housed the Royal Chapel of the Treasure of St. Januarius. So much art, so much sculpture, so much marble, so much gold! Although high Baroque Catholic architecture is not my taste, frankly I judge it as vulgar, one can't help but be in awe of the skills of these 16thC artisans who created these man-made miracles. Again, I'm outraged at the hugely disproportionate use of scarce resources used to house "God" rather than house mankind. The only way I can come to terms with these emotions is to consider these Cathedrals, Basilicas and great Mosques, as memorials to the craftsmen who built them. (You might note that I've excluded synagogues from that list but that's because after the fall of the second Temple the Hebrew houses of God have been very modest in comparison and many of the ultra-orthodox pray in *Stiebels*-Yiddish for small room. Nevertheless, even the greatest of cynics would have to agree that religious faith and the Bible stories have been the inspiration for some of the greatest works of art of all time.

For example, Giotto's frescos in the *Cappella degli Scrovegni* in Padua, transform a modestly sized chapel into a totally immersive work of art. Piero de la Francesco's "Baptism of Christ", Raphael's Madonna, Michelangelo's Sistine Chapel, Leonardo's "The Annunciation" and all the works of Rembrandt illustrating the scriptures, need no introduction. With the exception of much of Rembrandt's work, the Church was the most important source of patronage, but during the period of the Golden Age of Dutch art, patrons included the wealthy burghers of commerce.

Because the Jewish and Muslim faith banned naturalistic images of human subjects thought to be idolatrous, few famous paintings or sculptures can be found in their houses of worship. A notable exception is the synagogue at the Hadassah hospital in Jerusalem bearing the gorgeous stained-glass windows of Marc Chagall, illustrating the iconography of the 12 tribes of Israel.

## Why Am I a Jew?

Visual arts aside, we must not forget the rich legacy of music we have been fortunate to enjoy, composed by musicians inspired by their faith. My personal favorites are the requiems by Mozart and Verdi, Handle's Messiah, the hymn Jerusalem that starts with the words, "And did those feet in ancient times", with words by Blake and music by Hubert Parry, and most of all, Christmas Carols. In my youth I sang in a choir whose repertoire included all of those items in spite of the fact I wasn't Christian! I was determined not to deny myself these transcendental trips because of such an insignificant objection. After all we all believe in the same God; don't we?

Three years ago, I took one of the grandsons who lives in New Jersey, up to Cambridge for an interview at Emmanuel College where he'd hoped to study computer science in the next academic year. After I had escorted him to the Spartan cubicle where he was to spend the night, I took him on a tour of the College. At the side of the main quadrangle opposite the main entrance we noted flickering lights and heard a heavenly choir singing in perfect harmony. We crossed the quad and found ourselves in a chapel with a date across the portico reading 1667. It was a Sunday evening two weeks before Christmas and we had stumbled across a carol service. The Baroque architecture, the oxblood color of the polished wood of the choirstalls, the red collars on the white cassocks of the choir boys, the green tinsel covered fir tree and the painting of the holy family on the far wall, created a backdrop from which emerged the Christmas carol, "Hark the Herald Angels Sing". I found myself deeply moved and almost tearful; there is no secular or atheist equivalent. I will return to that theme later.

To my way of thinking, the greatest good that faith communities can offer is in building of communities. This is worth a chapter of its own.

# Chapter 6

## *A Question of Community*

EACH YEAR OUR LOCAL primary school (age 7–11) has an arts week in the Spring term. To help with the additional burden, the headmaster recruits local artists in the neighborhood to supervise the schoolchildren with their projects. I volunteer each time because I love teaching kids as much as I loved teaching undergraduates. Each year they have a theme. Five years ago, the theme was Rio de Janeiro and the Brazilian Olympics. That was easy. A year later, the theme was "Community". How can you explain such an abstract concept to children aged 7–11 and then guide them in the making of a picture to illustrate the concept? I spent a lot of time thinking this through and put together a PowerPoint presentation. I found it helpful to illustrate the concept in a multilevel, tree like, hierarchical model. At the base of this pyramid, we have a collection of nuclear families (grandparents, mother, father, children). Next level up is the extended family including uncles, aunts and cousins. With enough extended families who share the same genealogy you have a tribe. Up another level you may have a group of tribes who bond together because of common interests or shared belief systems. As an example, I asked the classes I was teaching to raise their hands if they supported Arsenal or Spurs (for those ignorant of the beautiful game, these are both premier league football teams in north London and are bitter rivals). This turned out to be an interesting experiment. Each class reacted the same way with a "Lord of the flies" moment. The youngsters supporting the Gunners (Arsenal) started booing those supporting Spurs and the Spurs supporters in return made rude gestures and screamed abuse at the Arsenal fans. I had to intervene to stop a riot. However, unintentionally I had made a point. A true community is made up of families and tribes who not only share common interests, common beliefs and common concern for each other. But as already described, tribes also go to war.

A village with a pub and a cricket pitch on the green may act as a community, a country like the UK governed as a Liberal democracy who chose to leave the community of the EU. Sadly, the illustrates the power of entropy that are tearing these communities apart, with Scotland seeking independence. Beyond Nation States there is another glue that bonds people together into global communities and that is Religion. Here is an extract from a lovely short essay by Matthew Syed that appeared in The Times on October 30 , 2017.

> *My parents used to host a Bible study on Tuesday evenings and a youth group on Sunday nights. Up to 20 people would crowd into our living room, sipping tea and sharing experiences. The church was not just a place of worship but a support network, a way to meet new friends and a key part of the community. The services were marvelous, too, not least because of the wonderful music. To this day, I often listen to Christian music in the car, mainly the hymns of Charles Wesley. I remember church with huge affection. I left not because I lost faith with the people, or the institution, but with the theology. If God is a fiction, as I came to believe in my twenties, what's the point? I just regret that I never quite found another forum so conducive to friendship and mutual support.*

## A Question of Community

In that one paragraph, Syed perfectly captures the point I want to make. The Church is not just a house of prayer it is also the center of a community that shares common beliefs and shares common concerns for all its members. On the village green, known as "Central Square", close to where I live in Hampstead Garden Suburb, there are two splendid churches. One is Anglican and is named after St. Jude and the other is the Free Church that takes all comers. The first is high Church the second is very laid back. Even though not a Christian I benefit in many ways by the communal work that they encourage. Every summer St. Jude's hosts the season of concerts we call the Proms and every New Year's Eve the Church organizes a party with a magnificent firework display as the clock strikes midnight. The Free Church supports the visual arts by hosting exhibitions with works by local artists as well as being the hub for the University of the Third Age (U3A). Everything about these Churches as well as our modest Quaker's meeting house is virtuous; our wider community would be poorer without them. We have a neighborhood tramp (hobo) named Tom, who wanders round the suburb talking to himself. Probably a burnt-out schizophrenic. He is filthy with long greasy hair and beard, fearsome in appearance but utterly harmless. He sleeps under the arches of the doorways of these places of worship, where food is left for him, he will also accept the gift of second-hand shoes. On a grander scale the London Diocese has opened night shelters for the homeless. This is a constant reminder to us that when the government social services fail, we can always rely on the Church to care for those who fall through the net. I know that there are secular organizations for the homeless in the UK, but the Church got there first. One block away from Central Square is Norris Lea Synagogue that has the largest Jewish congregation in NW London. The Hebrew for Synagogue is *Bet Ha' Knesett* which translates as House of Assembly rather than house of prayer. The Jewish community revolves around the Synagogue, but that is not simply a house of prayer, but also a meeting house and a center of learning. This community center takes care of the elderly and acts as a charitable foundation that looks after the sick and needy as well as raisings funds to support similar groups in Eastern Europe and Israel. We were privileged to belong to such a community and feel safe in its embrace at this time of crisis. We are also privileged to belong to a virtual community within Hampstead Garden Suburb that makes us feel like we are living in a village. Mutual support groups are popping up all over the place as we witness the very best of humanity emerging. At the same time, I worry about the invisible sub-groups of society who have nowhere to turn to. The homeless living on the street, the kids living in sink estates and most of all the aged lonely ones with no family nearby. At the very least we should subscribe to the charities to support those who inevitably fall through the government's safety net through no one's fault. Yet things are moving so fast on the final days that I'm writing this book, I've been overtaken by events. The government has decreed that all those citizens that are sleeping rough must be taken into temporary refuge by the local authority that has control of the pavements or doorways where they sleep.

The United Kingdom is now beginning to act like a community again, a valued collateral effect of the pandemic. As evidence for this, in addition to the 35,000 doctors, nurses and other front-line staff who came out of retirement to man the barricades, an additional 700,000 have volunteered to provide care and deliver food and medicine for those old or vulnerable folk who are judged at high risk and are already in strict isolation. That works out at one volunteer for two of those in personal lock down!

Further afield, a global village has been constructed, as all the wealthy countries in the world are collaborating in the science, testing and manufacturing the kits for identifying the antigens and antibodies for COVID-19, and working together to develop vaccines. The WHO has now turned its attention to the low-income countries in Sub Saharan Africa and the Indian subcontinent, who have virtually no adequate health care services at the best of times. Much is left to be done as we witness the unbelievable scenes in India at the time I'm writing, where the health service has collapsed, poor folk are dying on the pavement outside hospitals and all the crematoria are overflowing. There is of course another example of

## A Question of Community

the ugly side of religion when millions of Hindu faithful bathes in the "holy river" Ganges for a festival that happens every 12 years that appeared to have kick started the second wave.

These unified actions are not only for the benefit of our own self-interests but reflect the burgeoning of our instincts to perform small acts of kindness. This behavior has not been fueled by the fear of hell if they neglect their neighbor, or for the promise of heaven for doing good deeds, *no,* it's because virtue carries its own reward as Spinoza expounded 350 years ago.

# Chapter 7

## *Why Am I a Jew?*

*"Once I was young man now, I am an old man;
yet have I not seen the righteous forsaken, nor his seed
begging for bread."*

FROM THE LAST VERSE OF GRACE AFTER MEALS.

WHEN I WAS A young man, I was rescued from a period of doubt and skepticism about my faith after reading a very short, but very inspiring book by Edmond Fleg, entitled "Why I am a Jew", that was translated from the French in 1929. He dedicated his booklet "To my grandson who is not yet born". Now I am an old man I am experiencing fresh doubts as I have oft-times seen the righteous forsaken. So, I have changed the heading of this section from the assertion, "Why I am a Jew", to the question "Why *am* I a Jew?" (Note the emphasis on the second word)

As it would be a biological improbability of Biblical proportions, to dedicate my little book to a grandson yet to be born, I have chosen to dedicate it to my one granddaughter and eight grandsons; Ellie, Joshua, Raphael, Samuel, Zack, Leo, Theo, Joseph, and little Jake, who range in age at the time of writing from

## Why Am I a Jew?

24 to 12. I am truly blessed: but by whom? That is the question. In his introduction Fleg asks of his unborn grandson:

> When will you read what I have set down? About 1950, 1960? Will people still read in 1960? What form will the world then take? Will the mechanical have suppressed the spiritual? Will the mind have created a new universe for itself? Will the problems that trouble me today exist for you? Will there be any Jews left?

That was written in 1929 and since then the world has changed beyond the stretch of his imagination. People still read, but Fleg would find it difficult to believe that I'm reading his words on my iMac. The "*mechanical*" has led to the World Wide Web that is the platform for so-called social media that has facilitated the spread of the "*spiritual*" worldwide, like a virus. An evil interpretation of the *spiritual* has indoctrinated naïve young men and women with extremist ideologies that threaten the future of the founding values of the French State where he lived: Liberté, égalité, fraternité.

Yes, the problems that troubled Edmond Fleg, still exist and are if anything amplified today, 87 years later. And YES, there are Jews left but not for the want of trying by Hitler and the Nazis during the Second World War. The good news Edmund is that the Zionist dream was fulfilled when the State of Israel was established in 1948 but the bad news is that the country is surrounded murderous terror organizations that with a remarkable cognitive dissonance, denying the first Holocaust yet promising the second. There is also a global axis of evil whose ambition is to acquire nuclear weapons to fulfil this promise. Nuclear weapons? Sorry Edmond I forgot to mention that the atomic bomb was invented in 1944! This has the capacity of wiping out cities with populations of more than 6,000,000 repeating the holocaust with one strike.

So, who do I thank for my blessings? That is the question I will attempt to answer in the last pages of this book but leaving aside any opinions I might hold regarding the nature of God, I wish to explain how someone like me choses to identify himself as a Jew whilst challenging the bedrock of his faith.

## Why Am I a Jew?

It is facile to say, "Born a Jew, always a Jew" or even worse for those who haven't at first hand experienced the horrors of violent anti-Semitism, to glibly state, "well even if I were to deny I was a Jew there are plenty of others out there who will remind me of my origins." In any case, it's been said so many times before, that it loses its punch and becomes a cliché.

Edmund Fleg earned the right to make that point as he lived in Paris during the anti-Semitic riots linked to the Dreyfus affair. As did Stanislaw Lem.

> *I was a good student. Some years after the war, I learned from an older man who had held some position or other in the pre-war Polish educational system that when the I.Q.s of all high-school students were tested—it must have been around 1936 or 1937—mine was over 180, and I was said to have been, in the words of that man, the most intelligent child in southern Poland. (I myself suspected nothing of this sort at the time of the test, for the results were not made, known to us.) But this high I.Q. certainly was of no help in surviving the Occupation of the Generalgouvernement (to which administrative unit Poland had been reduced by the Germans). During that period, I learned in a very personal, practical way that I was no "Aryan". I knew that my ancestors were Jews, but I knew nothing of the Mosaic faith and, regrettably, nothing at all of Jewish culture. So, it was, strictly speaking, only the Nazi legislation that brought home to me the realization that I had Jewish blood in my veins. We succeeded in evading imprisonment in the ghetto, however. With false papers, my parents and I survived that ordeal.*

## GENETICS

Maybe I have no choice in this matter because it's coded in my genes. That suggestion implies that to be a Jew is to belong to a distinct race. Forgetting the "racist" overtones of this conjecture and sticking to the science, I believe there is no such thing as race. All members of the species *homo sapiens* are distantly related to each

## Why Am I a Jew?

other as we all came out of Africa more than 100,000 years ago. We don't even need to go back that far. Family trees do not go on branching in a symmetrical manner otherwise this planet would have been overwhelmed by our numbers. Even going back 3,000 years we can deduce that nearly everyone is related to everyone as distant cousins and almost everyone carries "Jewish blood". In his delightful and very readable book, *A brief history of everyone who ever lived*, Adam Rutherford describes the scientific evidence that nearly all Europeans carry some of the genetic information inherited from Charlemagne, the first Holy Roman Emperor.

The question I'm posing therefore, must be more focused, do I carry more "Jewish blood" than the average European? The answer is probably not as there is no specific genetic sequence that has been identified that can answer the question with a simple yes or no. There are however, three genetic traits that can narrow the search down in certain individuals.

The first concerns mitochondrial DNA (mtDNA) that is inherited through the female line of any family. There is good evidence now that there are 4 "matriarchs" in Jewish molecular genealogy. These are not the Biblical Matriarchs, Sarah, the wife of Abraham, Rebekah, the wife of Isaac, Leah and Rachel, the wives of Jacob. The 4 distinct mtDNA alleles are only found in about 50% of those who claim to be Ashkenazi Jews and are probably accounted for by a bottleneck phenomenon after a period of mass persecution in the distant past. In other words, the sudden shrinkage of the population left only four women with sufficient fecundity to found strong familial lines.

The other two interesting traits are indirectly of interest in my own family. I have three out of eight grandsons that consider themselves *Cohanim,* that is direct descendants of the first High Priest, Aaron brother of Moses. That sounds a bit far-fetched and is simply part of an oral tradition. Their father is Lewis Cohen who is the son of Rabbi Doctor Jeffrey Cohen who is also the son of one of the claimants of descent from the first High Priest. As it turns out there is a specific allele on the Y chromosome known as the Cohen modal haplotype that is found in 70% of those who claim this ancestry and in only 1.0% of a control population. I find this almost unbelievable but can't deny the science.

The third trait concerns the predisposition to specific diseases. There are several such afflictions that are common among those who claim to be Jews but the one of specific interest to me is the BRCA mutations that predispose to breast cancer. The so-called Ashkenazi mutation, BRCA I. (It is estimated from studies of mtDNA, that the founder of this mutation lived >3,000 years ago) These occur in about 5% of women who have 4 Ashkenazi grandparents and are associated with early onset and aggressive breast cancers. My mother died of breast cancer and my sister is a long-term survivor having been diagnosed at an early age. She has four daughters, and they were naturally very concerned, so my sister elected to go for genetic testing. Fortunately, she tested negative and as a result I have no more genetic proof that I'm any more Jewish than you are.

## ANCESTRY

Yet, when it comes to ancestry, well that's another story altogether. When a young man and woman get married in an orthodox synagogue, they are issued with a *ketubha* (marriage certificate) that is countersigned by two witnesses of behalf of the community. But, before they are permitted to marry under the auspices of an orthodox community, they must be able to produce copies of the *ketubhat* of their parents.

So, unlike the oral tradition of the *Cohanim*, there must be a written provenance of the couples' Jewish ancestry. This could then lead to an almost infinite regression of documentation. Sadly, as far as European Jews are concerned, many are descendants of holocaust victims, this documentary proof went up in flames. My family were fortunate because both sets of grandparents got out in time. On my father's side, they escaped the pogroms in Russia and Poland, by migrating to London in 1911. We also have written material that traces the Baums (Tree in German), all the way back to a *shtetl* in woodlands near Warsaw, where my great, great, grandfather looked after the forest belonging to some Polish aristocrat. They were dirt poor and shared their plot with the Roma. Imagine "Fiddler on the roof" and you'll get a clear picture.

The Anglo-Jewish community is very small, in the last census 270,000, with a genetic pool shrunken by the bottleneck of the Holocaust, which means that there is a degree of consanguinity and that accounts for the prevalence of the Ashkenazi mutations. As a result, we have the saying, that when you are introduced to a Jew born in the UK, if you haven't found out that you are distantly related after 20 minutes of conversation you should continue for a further ten!

So, like it or not I am a Jew, but why do I persist in defining myself as Jew rather than, as Johnathan Miller put it,—Jew-ish? "TRADITION!"- As Teviya the milkman sings in "Fiddler on the roof"; yes, but more than that, a sense of community.

## BELONGING TO A JEWISH COMMUNITY

As already described, community implies a group of people who share common values and common interests. The Jewish community revolves around the Synagogue, but that is not simply a house of prayer, but also a meeting house and a center of learning. This community center takes care of the elderly and acts as a charitable foundation that looks after the sick and needy as well as raisings funds to support similar groups in Eastern Europe and Israel. The members of my community share a common culture and similar tastes. Our culture has many threads, some can be traced back to biblical times, others to mediaeval times in central Europe and the Iberian Peninsula, the Yiddish culture of the Pale of settlement set up by the Empress Catherine the Great, the Golden Age in Germany and Austria before the Nazis, 20thC USA after the World War II and the modern state of Israel. These have conditioned us to have passionate interests in philosophy, science, psychology, poetry, literature, the visual and performing arts, the composition and performance of music and food. Often all at the same time.

## Why Am I a Jew?

A typical evening at the theatre would start by us scanning the auditorium to see how many members of the "tribe" we can recognize. If the answer is none my wife, then assures me the show can't be any good. If instead, we recognize any friends or family we gesticulate in code across the crowded room in a way that can be translated as, "Let's meet in the interval for a drink, have you eaten yet and did David get into Oxford?".

Sometimes the synagogue runs out of space leaving the wider community to extend or complement its role. My family is lucky to live in one of the most vibrant Jewish communities in the UK (London NW3/NW11). We have easy access to the splendid new arts and culture facility known as JW3. Although founded by Jewish philanthropy, non-Jews are welcome as members. Here we can attend lectures on the arts, history and literature and watch the latest movies in comfort, even if not specifically linked to Jewish topics. For example, in the year before lockdown, we had a lecture on Pierre Bonnard, that was the current the theme of a great exhibition at the Tate Modern. Another lecture that year, was by a brilliant historian, talking about Britain in the inter-war years, 1915–1939. Both theatres were packed to the rafters, mostly by members of the Third Age, still thirsty for education. They also hold classes in painting, bridge, languages (including Ivrit of cause), and the martial arts.

Another facility within easy reach, is Chai Cancer Care, a beautiful, well-equipped and well-staffed unit, providing aftercare, counselling and complementary treatments for those suffering from cancer that can include all their family members. Recently a new wing has opened to help-out with the load of palliative care at our local NHS, teaching hospital, The Royal Free. All this is paid for by charitable donations and a fund-raising annual dinner. It is this concept of community that has kept us alive. The late beloved ex-Chief Rabbi of the United Kingdom, Jonathan Sacks, recognized this and described the importance of communities of faith even for those who reject the faith. This he made clear in an essay he wrote for Standpoint Magazine in 2017, entitled "Cultural Climate Change", that I wish to quote from.

## Why Am I a Jew?

> *Darwin realized that in every single human society ever known, it is the altruists, not the survivalists, who are admired. For a group to survive, it has to have altruism among its members. When you've got a society of individualists who think mainly of themselves, it is poor in social capital. The classic work on social capital was written in our time by a great sociologist at Harvard called Robert Putnam. He is famous for his observation that more people are going 10-pin bowling in America than ever before, but fewer are joining teams and leagues. He called his book "Bowling Alone". That, for him, became the symbol of an individualistic society which is rich in individual life but poor in social capital. Poor in altruism, in other words. "Social capital does exist in America. But where will you find it? In churches, in synagogues, in temples, in houses of worship." However, the truth is that if you are a regular goer to church, synagogue or other place of worship, you are more likely to help a stranger in need. The best indicator is: do you or don't you go regularly to a house of worship? An atheist who went regularly to church is more likely to be an altruist than a deeply believing believer who keeps to himself.*

Lord Sacks might have been describing me in that essay but I haven't yet confessed to being an atheist. So, I choose to remain a Jew because of all the advantages eloquently explained in Lord Sack's essay but this decision is buttressed by two other benefits—I don't have to compromise my scientific integrity and the comfort I enjoy through ritual.

## MEDICAL HALACHA

> "I am a Jew because the faith of Israel demands no abdication of my mind."
>
> Edmund Fleg 1929

The expression "Medical Halacha" implies the study of medical ethics in relation to the Mosaic code of conduct. The book, "Jewish

## Why Am I a Jew?

Medical Ethics" by the late great Chief Rabbi Lord Jakobovits, has become something of a Bible for me. I first met Immanuel Jakobovits in the early 1980s when I was struggling with the knotty problem of informed consent for patients being recruited into randomized controlled trials (RCT) of treatment for cancer. At the time, I was professor of surgery at Kings College London and director of the Cancer Research Campaign clinical trials center. This was the first such center in the UK with a purpose-built unit, fully staffed to conduct RCTs. Nevertheless, the very notion of RCTs was considered controversial in those days. One of our fiercest critics, the then editor of the Journal of Medical Ethics, publicly accused me of advocating "human experimentation" and that I was no better than Josef Mengele. I was naturally extremely hurt by that accusation, so I booked an appointment to see the Chief Rabbi for advice. I found him very approachable, charming, and humane in his approach. He indulged me in a Talmudic debate that lasted well over an hour although I never considered myself a Talmudic scholar. He was very interested in my dilemma and clearly had not put his mind to this before. He asked for some time to deliberate and in return I invited him to address the members of my department at an open meeting a few weeks later. The meeting was packed out and all those present agreed that Lord Jackobovits' conclusions were rational, humane and ethical.

Medical ethics are not absolute codes of conduct that leapt fully formed and immutable from the heads of ancient sages in distant times, but as it turns out were first codified in the Pentateuch about 1,500 years before Hippocrates. Furthermore, Medical ethics demonstrate an uncomfortable plasticity with subtle variations emerging between different ages in history and between different ethnic and cultural groups. Medical ethics may be driven by the law of the land or by medical technology, but often, medical technology runs in advance of our capacity for ethical control and the law is a blunt instrument that may belatedly react to some of the worst medical abuses or as a late reaction to public outcry. All ethical codes of conduct for the practice of medicine have their foundation in philosophy and theology. For example, the Hippocratic oath, which is seldom recited today, probably emerged because of the teachings of respect for human rights and dignity at the birthplace of democracy in Athens 500 years before the Common Era. Much of the teaching of Plato and Socrates can be seen reflected in the teachings of Hippocrates. In contrast, contemporary medical ethics is heavily dependent on the teachings of Immanuel Kant of the 19 Century AD and his four "categorical imperatives"—autonomy, beneficence, non-malfeasance, and justice.

If only it was that easy! Contemporary medical problems illustrate the tensions that arise when there is often a clash of these categorical imperatives, particularly between distributive justice on one hand and the right to autonomy or self-determination on the other. Furthermore, some of these "categorical imperatives" clash with ethnic or religious minorities. For example, an absolute belief in the right to self-determination would allow suicide and assisted euthanasia that would be an anathema to orthodox Jewish teaching. The Jewish faith believes that life is of infinite value, and you cannot split infinity. Therefore, every moment of life is of infinite value, and therefore the individual or the doctor working on the individual's instruction must not do anything to shorten life. Jakobovits then surprised us all by saying it was a doctor's duty to explore more and better ways of prolonging life. Creation didn't stop after the 7 day, man was given the power of original thought that can improve upon creation and yes, Man should "Play God" if it was to improve the length and quality of life.

He recognized the ethical dilemma facing the clinical scientist concerning informed consent, but this informed consent must be a voluntary, unforced decision, made by a competent or autonomous person, based on adequate information and deliberation, to accept a specific treatment when fully cognizant of the nature of the treatment its consequences and risks. Furthermore, that there should be no fundamental difference between the information given to a patient in a clinical trial and that given in daily practice. In giving permission for a treatment the patient does not surrender his or her rights and failure to fully inform him of the hazards of intended treatment within or without a trial may leave him exposed to liability for criminal charges of negligence or battery. He understood that the RCT is the most efficacious way of minimizing risk to individuals, as well as advancing medical knowledge, breeding both good science *and* good ethics.

Following on that encounter we became very firm friends, an unlikely partnership between an orthodox Chief Rabbi and a secular Chief Sceptic. I was invited to join his "kitchen cabinet" that literally happened in Lady Jakcobvits' kitchen. These meeting took place maybe every six weeks, when a small panel of experts joined the Chief, to debate the latest medical ethical problem. I can only remember one area over which we couldn't reconcile our beliefs and that concerned homosexuality. We were very honored when Lord and Lady Jakobovits accepted the invitation to our youngest daughter's wedding at which his Lordship conducted part of the service.

❊ ❊ ❊

I want to give one more example of the halachic encouragement for doctors to "play God". In July 2016, on a blazing hot day in northern Israel where I was glad to stay indoors enjoying the air conditioning of the Dan Carmel hotel in Haifa, I found myself chairing a session at a scientific meeting on genomics. This meeting was convened by Professor Gadi Rennart chairman of the department of epidemiology at the Technion University. The meeting was set up to discuss the genetic predisposition to disease amongst the Jewish, Arab and Druze populations in Israel. One of the speakers in my session was Rabbi Professor Avraham Steinberg MD, a very famous expert of Medical Halacha. He is a majestic figure who stands tall in his long black coat and long grey beard, the very stereotype of the religious bigot. But one should never judge a book by its cover. Doctor Steinberg's task was to talk about the complex issues of in vivo fertilization (IVF), embryo selection and genetic engineering. His science was more up to date than mine, his attitudes were modern and liberal as once again, when challenged, he confirmed that it was the duty of medical scientists to improve on creation. The most interesting exchange came from another famous figure, Lord Robert Winston, an expert on in vitro fertilization, who spoke from the floor having earlier that day delivered the plenary address. Avraham Steinberg, in his talk, had given the halachic case in support of IVF and embryo selection. Robert Winston then alerted Dr Steinberg to some new work of his that was beginning to discover a disturbing increase in the incidence and early onset of a variety of medical conditions and wanted to know how this might modify his ruling. The good doctor Steinberg then replied, "Professor Winston, when your work is published, I will reconvene my panel of halachic experts who will study your new research and if needs be, modify our verdict accordingly". This is why I'm a great proponent of Jewish Medical Ethics, this code of conduct is not set in stone but responds to new scientific observations as they appear. The 10 commandments may have been chiseled in granite but their application today in practice of modern medicine is written in the archives of scientific journals.

## SUNDAY MORNINGS WITH RABBI LISS

It's very embarrassing to state in public, that Jews have won a disproportionate number of Nobel laureates. Since the Nobel was first awarded in 1901 approximately 193 of the 855 honorees have been Jewish (22%). Yet Jews make up less than 0.2% of the global population.

Richard Dawkins has this to say when asked if he had and explanation for this phenomenon: "I haven't thought it through. I don't know. But I don't think it is a minor thing; it is colossal to think more than 20 percent of Nobel Prizes have been won by Jews. Race does not come into it. It is pure religion and culture. Something about the cultural tradition of Jews is way, way more sympathetic to science than other faiths"

I think I have the answer to this dilemma Richard, it is indeed an aspect of our culture. Effectively Jews have been practicing scientific philosophy in parallel with moral philosophy from about 2,000 years ago. As an example consider the "Houses of Hillel and

Shammai", two schools of thought named after the sages Hillel and Shammai (of the last century BCE and the early 1st century CE) who founded them. These two schools had vigorous debates on matters of ritual practice, ethics, and theology which were critical for the shaping of the Oral Law and Judaism as it is today. The Mishnah mentions the disagreement of Hillel and Shammai as one which had lasting positive value:

> "A disagreement which is for the sake of Heaven will be preserved, and one which is not for the sake of Heaven will not be preserved. What is a disagreement that is for the sake of Heaven? The disagreement of Hillel and Shammai" (Pirkei Avot -Saying of our fathers)

One famous example of their heavenly disputations was the concept of a "white lie": Whether one should tell an ugly bride that she is beautiful. Beit Shammai said it was wrong to lie, and Beit Hillel said that all brides are beautiful on their wedding day. I was involved in this very debate only a few Sundays ago. Every Sunday morning, I join a select group of about 15 congregants from Highgate Synagogue that I recently joined, guided by our leader, a great sage himself, Rabbi Nicky Liss. Most Sunday mornings we gather to debate difficult issues in moral philosophy using the dialectal techniques of Rabbi Hillel and Rabbi Shammai. In other words, there is a thesis and an antithesis that are argued in the hope of arriving at a good-natured synthesis. But we go further, in that this *synthesis* does not become a dogma carved in tablets of stone but can change as circumstances change over time as long as they adhere to the fundamental principles of the laws that *were* carved in stone. For example, we also recently debated whether we should be allowed to hang out our washing to dry on the Sabbath for the neighbors to see, even though we did the washing before Shabbat came in? I had to remind Rabbi Liss that these days we have tumble dryers! I described a better example above, in the discussion between Lord Winston and Dr Steinberg concerning in-vitro fertilization.

This process is effectively what energizes scientific philosophy today and is close to the teachings of my favorite scientific

## Why Am I a Jew?

sage, Karl Popper, as expressed in his masterpiece, "The Logic of Scientific discovery".

No wonder Jews are good at science, it's hard wired in our brains, it's practiced around the dinner table on Friday nights, and it's taught in the *Yeshivas* (religious seminaries) were Rabbis start their careers.

## RITUAL

I love ritual and it resonates with my obsessive-compulsive personality. I think this might have been one of the motivators that encouraged me to train as a surgeon. The operating theatre has been likened to a Temple and the ritual of scrubbing up, gowning. and gloving and the laying on of sterile green drapes, echoes the rituals of the High Priest on Yom Kippur as described in Leviticus. I enjoy the rituals that mark the milestones of our lives and the cycle of the seasons. The celebrations around the birth of a new baby make a visit to the synagogue a joy. The *Brit* (Circumcision) ceremony is both solemn and joyous. The Bar mitzvah and Bat mitzvah are legendary for conspicuous consumption and an opportunity for the young man or young woman to show off his/her scholarship and singing voice for better or worse. If you live long enough you even have an excuse for a second Bar mitzvah at three score years + 13 i.e., 83. (I was 83 this year and planned my reading from the Torah followed by a *kiddush* but sadly the corona virus got there first)

The traditions of the marriage ceremony (*Chuppah*- literally canopy) are beautiful and always have me choking back tears. Part of the ceremony is the formal handing over and signing of the wedding contract (*ketubah*) that is often handwritten in ancient Hebrew letters and beautifully illustrated with iconic images of love, loyalty and faith. I've attended secular weddings and found those ceremonies completely lackluster.

And when your time is up the *lavoiya* (burial ceremony) and the *shiva* (the eight days of formal mourning at the home of the deceased), provides comfort for the mourners. Sadly, my oldest brother Geoffrey, died with the COVID-19 infection at the age of 92 in January 2021 and I was denied the comfort of rituals to help me through the period of mourning.

For every season, there is a Jewish festival often accompanied with banquets where special delicacies are eaten. (There is an old joke that suggests the whole practice of Judaism can be summed up as, "They tried to kill us, we survived, let's eat!") Of course, the exception is Yom Kippur when we fast for 25 hours from sunset on *Kol Nidre* (The eve of Yom Kippur) to sunset on the day of Yom Kippur, plus one hour "to be on the safe side". It goes without saying, that after the fast there is a feast and my dear wife used to enjoy catering for about 30 adults, both family and friends.

*Pesach* (Passover) is the Spring festival and often coincides with Easter which is no surprise because The Last Supper was thought to be the Passover feast. That feast is always stupendous and accompanied by *matza* (unleavened bread) and a mandatory four glasses of kosher wine. Seven weeks later is *Shavuot* (Pentecost) that celebrates the giving of the Law at Mount Sinai. For some reason, we eat cheesecake on that occasion. Then in the late summer comes *Rosh Hashanah* (the Jewish New Year) when we eat apples and honey and even the challah bread is sweetened. Yom Kippur is 10 days after that. The last of the high Holy days that spread out across September/October is *Sukkot* (The feast of Tabernacles) where we feast in . . . err, Tabernacles. Most of these are ramshackle sheds let in the rain, but the kids love building and decorating them. The best place to celebrate *Sukkot* is in Israel where it is truly a harvest festival, and the weather is at its best. Eating out at a friend's *Sukkah* is a delight as you enjoy the balmy, perfumed air and watch the stars twinkling through the palm tree branches that make up the roof.

Finally, *Chanukah,* the festival of lights that coincides with Christmas and the winter solstice. The ancient Greeks tried to kill us, we survived, let's eat . . . potato pancakes (*latkes)* and donuts. (don't ask)

*Why Am I a Jew?*

## SHABBAT (THE SABBATH)

The Christmas edition of the British Medical Journal in 2000, contained a feature where senior medical academics from round the world were invited to nominate the music they would wish for at their time of arrival and departure. Here is my contribution.

> *To be born to: Handel's Water Music, which is full of tunes that would accompany the breaking of the waters. To die to: "Etz chaim hi lamahazikim bah," the beautiful melody sung by the cantor as the Torah scrolls are returned to the ark on the Sabbath. The Hebrew translates as "The holy law is a tree of life to they who grasp it." My name also means tree, and the song would remind me of the fruit and branches left behind, which secure a degree of genetic immortality.*

The beauty of that moment just before the Torah Scrolls are returned to the Ark, is enhanced by the sight of the synagogue's collection of Torah Scrolls, standing in line and if the community is old and wealthy enough, up to three ranks of shelves, lined in white silk.

The *Sifre Torah* are dressed like royalty, with red or blue brocade coats, embroidered with gold thread, silver or sometimes gold breast plates and matching crowns on the spindles that carry the rolls of parchment. The Jews call themselves "The people of the book" and the books that are treated like a royal family, in every town and in every country, are the same, the scrolls of handwritten versions of the Pentateuch.

I have a nephew I'm very fond of, the second son of my youngest brother David, he trained as an artist and is skilled in calligraphy. He went on to train as a *sofer* (Hebrew scribe). He earns his living in part writing and illustrating *ketubha* and once was commissioned to write a *Sefer Torah*. That task took him the best part of two years.

The fourth Commandment (Exodus 20:8–11) goes as follows.

> *Remember the Sabbath, to keep it holy. Six days you shall labor, and do all your work; but the seventh day is a*

# Why Am I a Jew?

*Sabbath unto the Lord Your God, in it you shall not do any manner of work, you, nor your son, nor your daughter, nor your man-servant, nor your maid-servant, nor your cattle, nor your stranger that is within your gates; for in six days the Lord made heaven and earth, the sea, and all that in them is, and rested on the seventh day. Wherefore the Lord blessed the Sabbath day and made it holy.*

Note that is says nothing about going to watch Spurs play at home against Arsenal on Saturday afternoon, but otherwise it's unequivocal and one of the greatest innovations in the history of mankind. I introduce it here as the primary example of how religion can be the most effective way of building a sense of community. The Sabbath is a wonderful institution, I say this although I'm not *Shomer Shabbat* (Literally "guardian of the Sabbath). My late brother David was *Shomer Shabbat* and went on to become President of the Royal College of Paediatrics and Child Health after a successful career as Professor of Paediatrics at Bristol University. The only time he "broke" his strict observance of the Sabbath was when he was needed for an emergency at the hospital. Yet when it comes to a matter of life or death, it is mandated that those demands take precedent over the laws of the Sabbath. He died in office as PRCPCH at the age of 59 whilst leading a charity bike ride to raise money for the suffering of children in the Balkans' war.

We start the day of rest on Friday night at sunset and end it once we can see four stars in the sky on Saturday evening. Friday night is for me, the best reason to remain a Jew. I'm sure most of you have seen the play or the movie "Fiddler on the roof". Halfway through, Tevye's family gather in their finest clothes, Golda blesses the candles and together with her husband, sing the Sabbath prayer that starts with the words "May the Lord defend and protect you". Gradually the focus widens until we see every little household in the shtetl blessing the candles and joining in the song. Having watched the movie and several productions of the stage show (once sung in Polish on a visit to a conference in Warsaw), I still embarrass myself by quietly blubbing into my handkerchief at that point. I know that my great grandparents performed these rituals

## Why Am I a Jew?

in their tumble-down shacks in the Pale, as did my grandparents in a tenement in the east end of London during the first World War, as did my parents during the blitz in Whitechapel, as we have done most Friday nights surrounded by our family, and now, with the tables turned, guests of our children or our closest friends.

After the blessing of the candles the master of the household hold up a silver goblet and blesses the sacramental wine, takes a sip and passes it round the family for everyone to sip. The Shabbat challahs (two freshly baked braided loaves of white bread), that have remained hidden under their ceremonial cloth are exposed, are held aloft and blessed. The bread is then broken into pieces placed in a basket, sprinkled with salt and carried round the company by the youngest present. Fathers then bless their sons and daughter with hands on their heads, intoning; *"May God bless you and keep you. May God's light shine upon you, and may God be gracious to you. May you feel God's Presence within you always, and may you find peace."*

We all then sit down and get stuck into the traditional chopped liver, chicken soup with *kneidlach* (dumplings) and *lochsen* (noodles), roast chicken and roast potatoes. Whilst food is being served polite disputations concerning Synagogue politics, Westminster politics and Israeli politics, Arsenal's chances against Spurs the following day, or for those who prefer the oval ball to the spherical ball, Saracens chances against the Harlequins. To be heard the younger members of the family learn to speak louder and louder until, like an arms' race, until everyone is shouting at the same time. It's TRADITION!

These traditions bond the family and are shared throughout the world. Even though not "observant" in a conventional way, my wife and I never go out on a Friday night unless it is to bring in the Sabbath with friends or family. We keep a kosher kitchen out of respect for our more observant visitors (I will expand on this comment in the chapter on *Kashrut*). Even on cruise ships we will always find others to share with us *Kabbalat Shabbat* (the bringing in of the Sabbath). To be fully observant of the Sabbath takes more than a family dinner. Let me tell you a little anecdote that illustrates this complex behavior trait.

I live in Hampstead Garden Suburb (HGS) where there is a very high concentration of Jews, centered on the Norrice Lea Synagogue of the modern orthodox persuasion. HGS is a beautiful part of NW London nestling close to Hampstead Heath, rich with garden squares and costly real estate many of which are grade II listed buildings, rated as part of English heritage. I often walk from my home across the Heath to the old center of Hampstead village to catch the tube to central London. On this walk I only need to cross two roads, the rest being woodland: the first named Wildwood Road and the second The Spaniards. On this morning, as I approached Wildwood Road, I witnessed a strange sight. There was a long ladder leaned up against a tall lamppost and that ladder carried the weight of two orthodox Jews wearing high visibility tabards. I knew they were orthodox because of the head covering, long beards and curly sideburns. I politely asked them what they were up to and they replied that they were repairing the *Eruv*. "What's an *Eruv?*" I hear you ask to which I reply, "how long have you got?!" So, let me give you the shortened version.

The *Eruv* is a ritual enclosure that Orthodox Jewish communities construct in their neighborhoods as a way to permit Jewish residents or visitors to carry certain objects outside their own homes on Sabbath and Yom Kippur. An *eruv,* usually a discrete wire held aloft on poles, accomplishes this by integrating several private and public properties into one larger private domain, thereby avoiding restrictions on carrying objects from the private to the public domain on Sabbath and holidays. An *eruv* allows Jews to carry, among other things, house keys, tissues, medication, or babies with them, and to use pushchairs and walking-aids. The presence or absence of an *eruv* thus especially affects the lives of people with limited mobility and those responsible for taking care of babies and young children.

The *eruv* is closely monitored because if there should be a breech in the continuity of the wire, then it loses its power. That then explains my sighting of two rare birds up a lamppost on

## Why Am I a Jew?

Hampstead Heath. I have mixed feelings about this ritual boundary on the one hand it's *bonkers* but on the other hand it shows compassion. As holding irrational belief systems is not illegal, then anything that mitigates against any of the unfortunate consequences of these beliefs should be seen as compassionate. Within our community, we witness the consequences of our *eruv* on Saturday mornings when we find the forecourt of our synagogue looking like a baby buggy and Zimmer frame park. Curiously enough, amongst this detritus, you may also find the odd skateboard and scooter. I find this oddly satisfying.

I have one last thing to say about our community that relates to all Jewish communities around the world, from the Charedim on the extreme right wing to the Reform and Liberal communities on the extreme left wing, and that is the *Kiddush* after the morning service on *Shabbat*. Once the formal service is over, the congregation then moves across to the communal hall, to where tables are set out with wine, whiskey and light snacks. *Kiddush* literally means sanctification and this in turn refers to the blessing that Rabbi makes over the communal goblet of kosher wine. *Kiddush* after the morning service on the Sabbath, also implies something to eat. The tradition is that any family celebrating a wedding, Bar or Bat Mitzvah, or the recent birth of a child, funds the feast. On the tables, you will find little glasses of kosher wine (why little? -no one in the right mind would want to drink a large glass of kosher wine!), wee drams of excellent single malt whiskey, herrings, humus and pastries. It is frowned upon to boast about your wealth by over-providing on such occasions, but occasionally we are treated to a *cholent Kiddush*. On the Jewish Sabbath, you are not allowed to kindle a flame, even an electric spark is considered as breaking the 4 Commandment. So, back in ancient times some culinary Jewish genius invented a stew made up of beef, potatoes, beans, carrots and lentils, that could be slowly cooked over night from just before sunset on Friday, to be at its peak at 1.00pm on Saturday. This provided a hot meal on Shabbat in a cold climate and covertly provided at least one hot meal a week for the poverty-stricken congregants without shaming them in the process.

## Why Am I a Jew?

My childhood memories include waking up every Saturday morning to a house smelling deliciously of cholent. After walking home from *shul* (Yiddish for Synagogue) after morning service, I would look forward to gorging myself on my mother's stupendous stew and later that day, throwing up on the side-lines after secretly creeping out of the house for rugby practice at school.

Just as the Shabbat is welcomed in with a blessing over wine so is the new week is welcomed in at the end of shabbat with a lovely short service known as *Havdalah*. There are a triad of symbolic artefacts that accompany this service that are often fashioned out of silver, the wine cup, a single candle holder and an elaborate spice box. The cup of wine is for a blessing on the new week, the spice box is emblematic of a sweetly fragrant week and the single platted candle is held high to light the path. Lord Sacks described the legend of the exile from the garden of Eden as the precursor of this ceremony. The Bible tells us that Adam and Eve were created on the 6 day and that on the 7 day God rested. Adam and Eve were guilty of the first sin by eating of the fruit of the Tree of Knowledge. For that reason, they were to be expelled but God delayed their sentence until the end of the day of rest. Instead of sending them into darkness he relented and gave them a light to start their journey into the unknown.

### CHAREDI JEWS

The stereotypic Jew, that comes to mind amongst non-Jews, are those who are distinctive by their clothes. Then men hastening to and from the synagogue on Shabbat in Crown Heights New York, Stamford Hill in London, or the *Mea Sheraim* in Jerusalem, have long beards, *payot* (long sidelocks), big black hats or even tall fur hats (*shtreimels*), long black kaftans that some of the wealthy have tailored in silk, long black trousers that may or may not be tucked into black or white socks.

This apparel dates to the time of the Pale of settlement in Eastern Europe and the subtle differences are the uniform of these sub-cults, reflects the wardrobe of a great religious leader of the past, The Rebbe. Menachem Mendel Schneerson, known to many as the Lubavitcher Rebbe or simply as the Rebbe, was a Russian Empire-born American Orthodox Jewish rabbi, and the most recent Rebbe of the Lubavitcher Hasidic dynasty. He is considered one of the most influential Jewish leaders of the 20th century.

The women folk dress more modestly, they wear long dresses, woolen stockings, dresses that cover their neck and arms. Their head is covered by a snood or the *sheitel*, the wig women wear once they are married, and their hair has been shorn off. They live in closed communities and strictly adhere to the letter of the law from the Torah and its oral interpretations, the Talmud. Without any disrespect intended, they are very different to main-stream Jewry in Europe, America and even in Israel. They pose no threat to other Jews or their host countries, but they do pose a threat though to the secular Jews in Israel because they have great influence in the make-up of the governing party. I'll return to that when I discuss Spinoza's views of the separation of government and the "Church" in politics.

Those on the inside however are governed with a rod of iron and God help the ones who try to break away from their sect. As it happens two very popular television programs give a very fair and balanced view of life amongst the Charedim. These are Netflix's 'Shtisel' and *"Unorthodox",* a four-part Netflix adaptation of Deborah Feldman's 2012 memoir. Shtisel takes place in *Bnei Brak*, a town just east of Tel Aviv. A young man yearns for an older woman but must contend with the meddling of a domineering father. The father, a widower, is on the prowl himself, though he seems as captivated by the tasty dishes eligible women cook as he is with the women themselves. Meanwhile, his daughter painfully copes with a husband who has taken off on a business trip that cloaks a romantic fling. I identify with the young man, Kive, because his ambition is to become an artist and refuse to teach in his father's Talmud/Torah school. This series has become absurdly popular all over the world, not just amongst Jews but equally amongst gentiles. I've just watched the last episode of series three and want to go back to beginning again!

## Why Am I a Jew?

The main character in *Unorthodox* is Esther Shapiro, played by Shira Haas. She's a young woman from an insular community of Hasidic Jews in Williamsburg, Brooklyn, who are mostly descendants of Holocaust survivors. She's unhappy in an arranged marriage and asks her piano teacher to help her escape. "Shtisel" shows the Charedi in a better light than "Unorthodox". The latter is more three dimensional as in the good, the bad and the ugly. The ugly side is the hideous way young women are married off with the sole purpose of breeding. The most vivid theatrical device in this drama was the startling contrast between Esther's buttoned up life in New York with the mildly hedonistic lifestyle of the young musicians in Berlin. In a nightclub scene if men danced with men, they were gay couples whereas in New York all the men danced together to save them from the lust should they (God forbid) dance with someone of the female gender.

This reminds of the old joke of the Rabbi and his friend, a clergyman, sitting together at a Jewish wedding.

> Clergyman: *I note that all the men and women are dancing separately, why is that?*
> Rabbi: *The Torah teaches us that men must not touch women for fear of lust.*
> Clergyman: *But surely men and women must come together to increase the size of your flock.*
> Rabbi: *Of course! The Torah tells us to go forth and multiply.*
> Clergyman: *Does the Torah advise on how this intercourse should be conducted?*
> Rabbi: *The Talmud interprets the Torah's decree that the man must be on top.*
> Clergyman: *But what if there is a serious disparity in weight, could the wife go on top?*
> Rabbi: *If it's a question of life or death, yes.*
> Clergyman: *Understood, but could they also do it standing up?*
> Rabbi: *God forbid, it could lead to dancing!*

Joking aside, my relationship with the Charedi community in London, has been affable in the past. Because the community rarely read the national newspapers or watch TV, they are very naïve about health matters above and beyond the teachings in the

## Why Am I a Jew?

Talmud and the healthy advice of Maimonides. In the past I have been invited by leaders in the community for advice on individual cases and once was asked to address an audience of 300 women on the issues of breast cancer awareness.

Unfortunately, my respect for these over-zealous Jews has sunk to an all-time low, because of their refusal to adopt the government's advice on social distancing. They continue to assemble in large crowds for prayer. As a result, they overrepresent deaths from COVID-19 eight greater than the British population.

In contrast the modern orthodox Jewish community, that all our family and friends belong to, have adopted the strictest interpretation of social-isolation, and have organized social services to support the community at a time of threat. As I was writing earlier this year (2021), I should have been looking forward to *Pesach* (Passover) with my family, but the festival that evokes the exodus from Egypt following the 10 plagues, was cancelled because of only one plague.

# Chapter 8

## *Circumcision and Kashrut*

FROM THE VERY START I've written this book from my viewpoint of a rational scientist whose primary concern is the physical and psychological well-being of members of my species. I also share a concern for the unnecessary suffering of other sensate species. Although I can accept, and will demonstrate, that the spiritual needs of homo sapiens can enhance their physical needs and well-being, that will require the same quality of evidence that has determined the care of my patients with cancer. I will start with the ritual of circumcision and then go on to describe the laws of kashrut (kosher food) that includes the rules governing *shechita* (slaughter of animals)

### THE COVENANT OF CIRCUMCISION

> **Genesis 17** When Abram was ninety-nine years old, the LORD appeared to him and said, "I am God Almighty; walk before me faithfully and be blameless. Then I will make my covenant between me and you and will greatly

## Circumcision and Kashrut

*increase your numbers." Then God said to Abraham, "This is my covenant with you and your descendants after you, the covenant you are to keep: Every male among you shall be circumcised. You are to undergo circumcision, and it will be the sign of the covenant between me and you. My covenant in your flesh is to be an everlasting covenant. Any uncircumcised male, who has not been circumcised in the flesh, will be cut off from his people; he has broken my covenant."*

For the God fearing Jew, these instructions are unequivocal and appear early in the first book of the Pentateuch. It is estimated that one third of the world's population of men are circumcised. As well as it being mandated for Jews and Muslims it is also commonplace amongst Coptic Christians, the Ethiopian Orthodox church, in the Philippines, many African tribes and the Australian Aborigines. The fact that this ritual is unexceptional across the world does not satisfy my challenge. I wish to weigh up the pain inflicted on a baby boy at 8 days, the safety of the procedure and the putative health benefits that might justify or challenge the continuation of this ritual as the entry criteria for membership of the Jewish tribe. I am not concerned about other faiths and tribes as I think that is none of my business. In saying that I must emphasize that in no way can we speak of circumcision in the terms of female genital mutilation. To make such comparisons is malicious.

I think I can speak with authority on the subject from three points of view, I have been circumcised, my son and eight grandsons have been circumcised and in the years I was working as Professor of Surgery at Kings College Hospital in southeast London, I provided a service for the local Muslim population whose boys were circumcised at any age up until puberty.

To say I have an eclectic collection of books in my study, is an understatement. One shelf is designated for antique or curious books on anatomy and surgery. Amongst this crowd is a small collection of books that came to me after the death of a surgical friend and colleague. Oddest of them all is the smallest book I possess, measuring 10x17cm and holding 60 pages. It is entitled "The

Surgery of Ritual Circumcision", by Dr Jacob Snowman, first published in 1904 at the price of 7s/6d. It is a handbook for *Mohelim* in training. A *Mohel* is a man certified to conduct the *Brit Milah* (ritual circumcision) who might be a layman, a rabbi or a qualified doctor. Page1, Chapter 1, contains this admonition.

> It is essential that those who perform ritual circumcision should be familiar with the elementary teachings of the Aseptic System of surgery which is now adopted even in the most trifling surgical proceedings.

Later on he goes on to state;

> The natural protective power of the body against infection is diminished when infants are premature, suffering with jaundice, sickness or diarrhea. In these circumstances the circumcision must be postponed. (i.e., beyond 8 days)

In addition, the ritual should not take place at any time if there is a family history of abnormal bleeding such as hemophilia.

You may wonder what was so remarkable about that, even if published 120 years ago.

What I find worthy of comment was not the fact that Dr. Snowman was giving advice based on knowledge from the time of Lord Lister in the late 19thC, this guidance is in fact an interpretation of the laws laid down in the *Mishna* written by rabbis about 200CE.

The most extraordinary component of the ritual, that some may find disgusting, is the *Metzitzah,* whereby the *mohel* spits on the wound. According to Dr Snowman, this should now be performed through a glass tube containing a piece of cotton wool.

All the above suggests that 1,800 years the rabbi/doctors knew something about the anti-bacterial properties of saliva. As a result, the procedure is very safe and compares favorably with operations performed by surgeons like me in NHS hospitals.

Having persuaded myself that the procedure is safe, what might be the benefits and harms in the short and long term. First, we must consider the suffering of the baby. Tradition allows mild sedation by offering the child sips of kosher wine sucked from a

## Circumcision and Kashrut

gauze dressing. The knife is sharp, and the cut is swift, and the baby is often unaware of what has happened. The one who suffers most at that point in time is the mother. Changing the dressing must be carefully done as that can hurt but again the tradition is to put oil or cream on the dressings so that they don't stick. Short lived pain is seldom remembered. When I was a young surgeon in southeast London, I often had to deal with the victims of knife crime, and they were often unaware of the assault until they saw the blood soaking through their garments.

I would now like to discuss the short term and longer-term consequences of circumcision. The condition "phimosis" describes the tightening of the meatus at the tip of the prepuce (foreskin). This can be congenital or acquired. It is acquired if smegma (sebaceous secretions from folds in the skin under the foreskin) accumulates and leads to chronic infections that scar the apex of the foreskin. These infections can be acute and painful and are then called balanitis that might require an emergency circumcision. All of this can be avoided by elective circumcision but also by hygiene using cotton wool buds to clean under the prepuce. In the past, circumcision was suggested as a way to lower penile cancer risk. This was based on studies that reported much lower penile cancer rates among circumcised men than among uncircumcised men. But in some studies, the protective effect of circumcision wasn't seen after factors like smegma, and phimosis were considered. In the Western world, the risk of penile cancer is low even among uncircumcised men. Men who aren't circumcised can help lower their risk of penile cancer by practicing good genital hygiene. Circumcision has no impact on sexuality or intercourse. I'm unaware of any examples in this country where an adult male has taken his parents to court because of circumcision performed when they were able to give consent, impacting on the sexual life.

When it comes to the spread of HPV and the risk of cervical cancer in their partners, there is good evidence that in countries where there is a high incidence of this disease like sub-Saharan Africa, there is a protective effect for circumcision. The same applies to the spread of HIV/AIDS. Three randomized controlled trials (RCTs) of circumcision in (largely young) HIV-negative adult males were initiated in three different countries in Africa. In each case, the trial was stopped early because the results were so conclusive—demonstrating that circumcision has anything between a 50% and a 75% protective effect against HIV infection in men—that it was considered unethical not to offer circumcision to the control group in advance of the planned trial end date. Again this is irrelevant in resource rich parts of the world including those with established gay communities because genital hygiene can achieve the same outcome. I think the last word on this topic can be left to the Jewish Medical Association (UK). I'm one of the founder members of this organization. A few years ago, the Board of Deputies asked us to come up with an opinion on the pros and cons of ritual circumcision. After a well-mannered debate amongst the membership, that include a significant number of orthodox practitioners, we came up with this measured conclusion.

> *The only reasons for observance of this fundamental Jewish law are religious and cultural. Whilst we are aware of media reports of positive medical implications, such reports are not relevant to the Jewish motivation. Equally there is no evidence to suggest that there are any specific negative effects of the procedure. Millions of Jews and non-Jews have been circumcised worldwide, over many centuries without any documented major medical complications.*

## KASHRUT AND SHECHITA

*Kashrut* are the laws governing what can and what can't be eaten on a kosher diet.

Shechita applies to the laws governing humane slaughter of the animals that might be included in kosher cuisine. I will start with kashrut with an abbreviated extract from Leviticus that gives you an idea of the breadth and complexity of this subject.

## Circumcision and Kashrut

# Leviticus 11

> The LORD spoke again to Moses and to Aaron, saying to them, "Speak to the sons of Israel, saying, 'These are the creatures which you may eat from all the animals that are on the earth. Whatever divides a hoof, thus making split hoofs, and chews the cud, among the animals, that you may eat. Nevertheless, you are not to eat of these, among those which chew the cud, or among those which divide the hoof: the camel, for though it chews cud, it does not divide the hoof, it is unclean to you. The rabbit also, for though it chews cud, it does not divide the hoof, it is unclean to you; and the pig, for though it divides the hoof, thus making a split hoof, it does not chew cud, it is unclean to you.
>
> 'These you may eat, whatever is in the water: all that have fins and scales, those in the water, in the seas or in the rivers, you may eat. But whatever is in the seas and in the rivers that does not have fins and scales among all the teeming life of the water, and among all the living creatures that are in the water, they are detestable things to you. Whatever in the water does not have fins and scales is abhorrent to you.

These detailed guidelines go on and on and cover birds and insects. Some of the species listed have Hebrew names that have yet to be translated. In the end apart the obvious porcine and crustacean prohibition, the lists are so long that the very orthodox amongst us have an app on their smart phones, "Is it Kosher?".

There is no doubt that these laws were based on concerns for health rather than for religious reasons. Consider how primitive hunter/gatherer tribes of the stone age learnt, by trial and error what plants and fruits were poisonous. At a more sophisticated scale this approach must have applied to wider health concerns amongst the nomadic shepherd tribes wandering through the deserts and pastureland in the pre-biblical era about 5 millennia ago.

In early days and in primitive communities to this day, pork was judged unclean because of the risk of transmission of disease. These include tape work and certain viruses. With modern husbandry this should no longer apply so the admonition against pork is now associated with the very identity of being Jewish or for that matter, Muslim. The long history of Jewish martyrs going to their deaths for refusing to eat pork, strengthens that belief. None of my family or friends, who identify as Jewish, yet consider themselves secular, eat pork as far as I know.

This does not apply to shellfish, where the health hazards remain. I will illustrate that with two anecdotes. Many years ago, I was one of the faculty of a well-known teaching course on oncology, that took place every year in Miami, Florida. The traditional faculty dinner took place at the iconic "Joe's Stone Crab" restaurant, even though the organizers and half the visiting faculty were Jewish. These stone crab look hideous and hazardous, so I was always provided with an alternative. One year the whole faculty apart from me, went down with dysentery. I ended up delivering 6 lectures instead of one.

10 years ago, I had an attack of angina when rushing between terminals in Vienna trying to get home from a lecturing engagement in Warsaw. I saw a friendly cardiologist the next day who arranged for me to have a coronary artery angiogram. Just before the injection of contrast medium by the radiologist a few days later, I was asked if I was allergic to shellfish. I said I had no idea as I'd never eaten shellfish, why do you ask? He then explained that an ingredient of the radio-opaque liquid contained an allergen that cross reacted with crustacean protein. He went ahead and completed the procedure and yes, you've guessed, I am very allergic to shellfish and ended up on high doses of cortisone. You eat shellfish at your peril with the risk of dysentery or severe anaphylactic reaction.

I want to finish the section by describing another critical concept of kashrut; the laws prohibiting the mixing of milk and meat when we eat and avoiding contamination of milk and meat dishes in the kitchen. This prohibition is derived from the verse, "Do not cook a kid in its mother's milk." This verse appears in the Torah three times, twice in Exodus (23:19 and 34:26) and once in Deuteronomy (14:21). Unlike the laws governing the foods that may or may not be eaten, this one sentence is open to all sorts

## Circumcision and Kashrut

of interpretation. As a rational medical scientist my first concern is hygiene and health. None of the reasons given by the rabbis are fully satisfactory and it is clear that these practices fall into the category of traditions that have no logical reason and remain one of many of the commandments in the Torah that are beyond my comprehension. (Since writing this, my friend and colleague, Professor David Stone, suggested that these laws were a reminder that storing meat and milk together in Biblical times, might have had the risk of causing dysentery, with the milk acting as a culture medium for bacteria) That doesn't mean I object to them, as at first glance they couldn't do much harm. What worries me though is that the orthodox take this to extremes that I find absurd and for the poor amongst us, impossible to afford.

I grew up in an orthodox home and had a happy childhood. My mother was tireless in her efforts to maintain a kosher home. Not only did we not eat dairy of meat dishes at the same time, but we also had to wait 3 hours between them. Ultra-orthodox Jews believe the gap should be 6 hours in case, G-d forbid, they meet each other in the mid gut. My parents had four sets of cutlery and dishes (*milchich and flieschich*), two for everyday use and an extra two, kept in the attic for the Passover not only to avoid mixing meat with milk but also the double whammy of mixing leavened with unleavened. My very rich friends in Hampstead Garden Suburb might even have two dishwashers and there are even richer families that have two kitchens, one for milk and one for meat. I've never encountered an ultra-orthodox Jewish family wealthy enough to have four kitchens, but those who can afford it take their whole family to Israel for the 8 days of Passover.

Many, many, years ago, when I was a *smartarse* teenager, I took part in a debate about this topic at a Jewish youth group linked to my synagogue in Birmingham. To this day I remember the shock and horror of the rabbi chairing the debate as I exposed my heresy.

Those debating in favor of the motion that "this house believed in the laws of kashrut", argued that the laws protecting us from breaking the laws of the holy Torah, were like concentric

## Why Am I a Jew?

walls protecting us from falling into a snake pit. I argued that life was a journey through green pastures with hazards of snake pits along the way but wouldn't a ring of barbed wire and a red notice reading, "DANGER VIPER PIT" be just of good, freeing my pathway through life from too many obstructions. To this day I stand by what I said but I feel shame in that I upset so many of my friends and showed disrespect to my beloved rabbi and mentor.

Shechita is the Jewish humane method of slaughtering permitted animals and poultry for food. It is the only method of producing kosher meat and poultry allowed by Jewish law. Unlike circumcision, there is no ritual involved in shechita. With that definition my task is much easier; is shechita humane?

When I was a little boy of 7 or 8, we had a black cat named Lucky. I confess to tormenting that cat who wasn't so lucky. Like many little boys that age, I like to "experiment" with animals. One experiment was to determine the weight of stones on top of an upside-down pail, to keep Lucky imprisoned. I'd just finished calculating to threshold beyond which the cat could not escape, when my mother called me in for tea. Needless to say, I forgot about the trapped cat. Poor Lucky was trapped in that prison for 24 hours before a kindly neighbor heard his cries and alerted my parents. I was mortified by that experience and as you can see it has haunted me to this day.

I do not anthropomorphize animals, but I strongly believe they should not be hurt or tortured for the benefit of man's hunger or sport. I am not virtue signaling by saying that for I truly believe that there is enough pain in the world without promiscuously adding to this sum of suffering. I also believe that indulging in causing pain to animals, desensitizes and brutalizes mankind. It is but a short step from torturing animals to the dehumanizing minorities within a community who re then treated like animals. Thus, it was with the Nazis and the Jews.

I can fully understand and sympathize with vegetarians who take this a step further, yet I believe that we have descended from the hunter/gatherer tribes of the stone age. In proof of that we have two types of teeth, the incisors, and the molars. The incisors cut and the molars chew. It is natural for us to desire meat in our diet, and we have evolved to the top of the food chain. I'm therefore left with the task of persuading *myself* that shechita is humane.

I had not given much thought to this until about 30 years ago. At that point in time the Jewish community in the UK were under attack by an animal rights group over, what they called, "ritual" slaughter. The Rabbi of my community invited me to lead an investigation into the claims of this anti-shechita movement. At stake was the very future of the Jewish community in the UK. If a populist political party adopted this as part of their political platform and they came to power, then all orthodox Jews might have to emigrate. I warned the community that I would be guided by scientific principles. I defined three areas of enquiry:

1. Are animals treated humanely in a kosher abattoir?
2. At any time would the animal experience pain?
3. Would loss of consciousness be instant?

The Biblical sources listing the laws and practices of *shechita* are scattered throughout the Torah (Pentateuch), the Talmud (written commentaries elaborating on the 5 books of Moses) and the Mishna (oral traditions) codified by the learned rabbis about 200 CE. I never went to yeshiva (college for studying Torah, Talmud, and Mishna), so I had difficulty putting this section together. I've already described the sections in Leviticus that define those animals that can be included in a kosher diet, but these paragraphs are pre-empted by two lines in Genesis 9:3–4.

> *Everything that lives and moves about will be food for you. Just as I gave you the green plants, I now give you everything.*
>
> *But you must not eat meat that has its lifeblood still in it.*

Verse 3 is amusing as it is seriously modified in Leviticus 11, but verse 4 is critical as it is the law that insists the animal is exsanguinated after slaughter. This has led to the modern practice of rotating the carcass of the beast after the throat is cut, to allow the blood to drain under the force of gravity. There is little else in the Torah that provides additional guidance.

The Talmud and the Mishna provide more and more details of the procedure of shechita prominent amongst which is the prohibition of causing pain to animals. A good example can be found in—Tza'ar Ba'alei Chayim—(Talmud B.M. 32a)

Ultimately it was left to polymath, Moses Maimonides (1135–1204), to bring some order to these scattered instructions. "Since the desire of procuring good food necessitates the slaying of animals, the Torah commands that the death of the animal should be the easiest. It is not allowed to torment the animal by cutting the throat in a clumsy manner, by piercing it, or by cutting off a limb while the animal is still alive (*Guide of the Perplexed* III:48)."

Coming to the present day, it is only a Jew specially trained for shechita—a *shochet*—can perform shechita. He is required to study for several years and is examined, in theory and practice, in the laws of shechita, animal anatomy and pathology. He serves an apprenticeship with an experienced shochet before becoming fully qualified. Shechita is performed with a surgically sharp instrument, which must be perfectly smooth without the minutest notch or irregularity. The shochet constantly examines the instrument to ensure this standard is maintained. The frontal structures at the neck of allowable animals, including the trachea, esophagus, the carotid arteries and jugular veins are severed in one rapid and uninterrupted action causing an instant drop in blood pressure in the brain. This abrupt loss of pressure results in the immediate and irreversible cessation of consciousness and sensibility to pain. I've already described how a cut with a very sharp blade is not painful at the time. If this is a simultaneous event to stunning (loss of consciousness) then the procedure can be judged humane. English law defines "stunning" as "any process which causes immediate loss of consciousness which lasts until death" [The Welfare of Animals (Slaughter or Killing) Regulations 1995 Part I, regulation 2 (1)]. Shechita conforms to this requirement. In conventional abattoirs in the developed world stunning is achieved by a captive bolt gun (a steel bolt is shot into the skull at the front of the animal's brain)

## Circumcision and Kashrut

or electric shock (electrodes are clamped to the animal's head/heart and the animal is electrocuted.) Neither of these modalities are fool proof. In fact, they are open to abuse. The Times on the 30 of April 2021, published a leading editorial entitled, *The Times view on animal welfare failings: Cruel Country Footage showing a farmworker hammering pigs to death provides further evidence of serious problems in the industry.*

Finally, without relying on biblical sources or my subconscious prejudices, there are scientific publications that confirm the loss of neurophysiological impulses in the brain follow within seconds, the fall in blood pressure to the brain after suddenly emptying the venous return from the cerebrovascular supply to the organ of consciousness. A recent example comes from the work of Dr Stuart Rosen MA, MD, FRCP, from the Faculty of Medicine, Imperial College, London, concluded that: *shechita is a painless and humane method of animal slaughter.*

Not only do I think shechita is humane I think it is more humane that procedures approved in all other non-Jewish abattoirs.

# Chapter 9

## *Why I Am a Zionist?*

I THINK I'VE ALWAYS been a Zionist even before I understood the meaning of the word. My mother was born in London, but my father was born in Warsaw in 1901 when it was part of Russia. His family left to come to the UK in 1912. Although they were most likely economic migrants, he told me scary stories about the pogroms and how they had to barricade themselves into their home whenever the Cossacks came to visit. In April 1945, when I was 8 years old, my parents took me to the cinema to see Walt Disney's Fantasia. What they hadn't anticipated was the content of the Pathé newsreel that preceded the main film. The 11 armored division of the British Army had just liberated the Bergen-Belsen concentration camp and the images were terrible. My mother tried to rush me out of the theatre, but I kept looking back. The pictures of heaps of naked corpses being shoveled into pits by bulldozers, haunt me to this day. The music of Mussorgsky's "A night on the bald mountain", one of the themes in Fantasia, is still associated with the mass murder of the Jews by the Nazis, in my mind. I was vulnerable young boy, so the scene was set for a lifetime of feeling

## Why I Am a Zionist?

insecure, with the pogroms in Russia and Poland in the early 20 C and the Holocaust in Nazi Germany and all European countries of the third Reich. My father was a Zionist, and when I was 11, I joined a Zionist youth movement, Habonim. *Ha'bonim* is Hebrew for builders and in many respects, it was very much like the cub scouts, with a blue rather than green roll neck jumper, striped kerchief, toggle and colorful efficiency badges on the upper arms of the of the sweaters. We were organized into platoons, marched like soldiers, and went on camping holidays where we played field games. I reached the rank of *s'gun rosh gedud*, deputy leader of the platoon, and wore my chevrons with pride.

In retrospect I guess we were being brain washed into a militaristic, left wing, irreligious type of Jew, who would make *Aliyah* (Hebrew for going up or migrating) to Israel to join a kibbutz, plough the land and grow oranges, once we were adults. Although most of us grew up to become doctors, lawyers, and accountants, most of us tended to be left leaning in our politics but not to the extreme of collectivism as exemplified in the kibbutz movement. So, you see that I was one of the four substrata of the Zionist movement, left leaning irreligious rather than left leaning religious, or right leaning either way. If I remember correctly there were Jewish youth movements for each of these paths of indoctrination.

As I grew up, like most of my generation, I became obsessed with the holocaust and read any fiction or non-fiction book on this subject, that I could get my hands on. This habit continues to this day. One of the most recent books I've read of this genre was "The Kindly Ones" a doorstep of a book by Johnathan Littell, translated from the French. The story is told from a Nazi's perspective. Dr Max Aue is a family man and owner of a lace factory in post-war France. He is an intellectual steeped in philosophy, literature, and classical music. He is also a former SS intelligence officer and cold-blooded assassin. He was an observer and then a participant in Nazi atrocities on the Eastern Front, he was present at the siege of Stalingrad, at the death camps, and finally caught up in the overthrow of the Nazis and the nightmarish fall of Berlin.

His world was peopled by Eichmann, Himmler, Göring, Speer and Hitler himself.

As well as the books, the cinema and theatre, I've also visited the "top" holocaust memorial museums in the world. These included at least three visits to Yad Va'Shem in Jerusalem, as well as those in Berlin, Washington, and Los Angeles.

The children's memorial in Jerusalem is unique. It is hollowed out from an underground cavern, as a tribute to the approximately 1.5 million Jewish children who were murdered during the Holocaust. Memorial candles are reflected infinitely in a dark and somber space, creating the impression of millions of stars shining in the firmament. The names of murdered children, their ages and countries of origin can be heard in the background.

Everything I had learnt about the mass murder of Jews from the time of the Roman crucifixions, the bonfires of the Spanish Inquisition and the gas chambers of the Nazis, had served to strengthen my belief in the need for a Jewish Homeland and a right to self-defense.

In 1963, having qualified as a surgeon, I made *Aliyah* to Israel and was appointed as a junior assistant in a newly rebuilt hospital in the center of the Jezreel valley, in the charmless town of Afula, midway between Nazareth and Tiberias. I arrived in Israel with "no baggage" and great optimism for my future. I had a rudimentary knowledge of *Ivrit* (modern Hebrew) and could understand what it must feel like for a migrant arriving in a foreign land and being snubbed or patronized for your poor grasp of the natives' language. However, I learnt rapidly on the job by being thrown in the deep end.

The demography of the region was very interesting. Orthodox Christians from Nazareth, Arab Muslims from the neighboring villages, Jewish pioneers from the surrounding kibbutzim and the new immigrants from the civic housing projects in Afula Ilit, mainly from north Africa. Contrary to popular belief these days, there was no suggestion of prejudice or "apartheid", as the percentage of doctors and nurses reflected the local population apart from the ill-educated new immigrants. There were many high

## Why I Am a Zionist?

points during my sojourn in Israel. I made friends with a young Arab doctor was often an honored guest at his parent's home in a nearby village. I was seconded for a while as the only surgeon at the Scottish Mission Hospital in Nazareth, where I had to carry procedures for the first time with a nurse holding open a textbook at the right page. I once had to deal with gunshot wounds after fedayeen from the Golan heights, raided a farm at the border with Syria. I had to give evidence to the blue helmets of UNIFIL, who as usual did nothing of value to stem the violence. Without doubt the most rewarding experience of my time in Israel was when I volunteered to act as a medical officer at the archaeological dig at Masada overlooking the western bank of the Dead Sea. Digging up artefacts buried since the fall of the second Temple in 70CE, discovering copper coins bearing primitive Hebrew lettering and symbols of worship in the Temple and ostraca bearing words in ancient Aramaic, strengthened my sense of bonding to this arid wilderness.

Sadly, after the best part of two years, I returned to the country of my birth prompted by my loneliness away from my loving family, and the lack of career prospects. There were too many surgeons in Israel and those born in the country had priority over me for promotion. It took me about another two years to re-establish my career and eventually I was appointed as Professor of Surgery at Kings College Hospital at the age of 43. There were no impediments put in my way for promotion because of my religion and love of Israel. With age and maturity, I began to doubt the value of my obsession with the holocaust. I even had the temerity to question the value of Holocaust museums that must tread a very delicate path between a dignified memorial and (if you'll forgive me) a theme park. I think the ones I've visited do get it right, but I look upon it as a supplement, a visual aid, for what can be better achieved by reading the best literature on the history of the Jews in 20thC Europe. I then reached a point in my life, round about the age of 70, when I started to believe that antisemitism was a thing of the past in the UK. I remember a dinner party with a group of Jewish friends who were banging on about minor incidents that might just about be described as antisemitism yet compared with what the Windrush generation were suffering, were mere needle pricks. I smugly announced that never had I encountered antisemitism and that they were all being hypersensitive. Events in the last few months in the spring of 2021, has proved me wrong. Between 2009 and today the borderline between anti-Zionism and antisemitism has become increasingly indistinct. I end this chapter by reprinting a letter I sent to an old classmate of mine not long ago that illustrates the drift from anti-Israel beliefs, to anti-Zionism and finally to full grown antisemitism as sure as the wasp appears by metamorphosis in two steps from larva to pupa.

## LETTER TO A DECENT FAIR-MINDED ENGLISH PHYSICIAN

Dear Barry,

The answer to your question is a simple Yes. In my opinion many of the actions of the Stern gang and the Irgun marked them out as terrorist organizations. Having conceded that point I'm not sure I understand the purpose of your question unless the intention was to conjure up a moral equivalence between terrorist groups active in the 1940s with the actions of Hamas today. If that was indeed the hidden meaning of your question, then let me elaborate a response based on my recent experiences in Israel and my in-depth knowledge of the history of the troubles in the Middle East. My delay in responding was because I've been in Israel for the last 8 days as a delegate to the 100th anniversary celebration of the Israel Medical Association (IMA). The first day was spent in Tel Aviv, center of the prosperous coastal region, the second day at Beersheba in the south, the third in Jerusalem in the eastern Judean mountains and the last in Afula in the north near the Sea of Galilee. Each region has different problems and different demography. Tel Aviv is populated largely with white secular Jews, Beersheba is home to poor new immigrants from North Africa, the Yemen and Russia together with a large population of Bedouin. Jerusalem has the highest concentration of bearded and

## Why I Am a Zionist?

black-hatted Orthodox Jews, whilst in the north there are the largest concentrations of Israeli Arabs and Druze.

On our visit to Jerusalem we paid homage to the victims of the holocaust at Yad Vashem. Many of the delegates were senior officials from medical associations round the world including the president of the World Medical Association (WMA). Yad Vashem is not for the faint hearted as it describes in meticulous details the origins and mechanisms for "the final solution" of the Jewish problem. At the end of the visit the presidents of the WMA and IMA laid a wreath in the hall of remembrance following which a cantor sang the haunting *Kaddish* prayer for the 6M dead. So, what has this to do with your question and what has the holocaust to do with the poor suffering Palestinians in Gaza? That was then this is now and I suppose that like many decent western liberals you are a bit bored with the Jews banging on about the holocaust as if that has anything to do with the current upheaval in the Middle East. Maybe I unfairly stereotype you but, in any case, stay with me because the next bit is interesting.

Everyone knows about the "mechanics" of the final solution, it was simply industrially scaled up Rentokil, an efficient way of cleansing the house of vermin although it took them a couple of years to figure out the best way of doing it. In the UK we get exercised by the culling of badgers with gas so how could the Nazis get away with the culling of Jews? Now that's the key question and that's probably why nice decent western liberals like you have a duty to visit Yad Vashem, where they explain the necessary precursor steps to genocide, exceptionally well. This is how it works. First you need to delegitimize the minority group in question and second you must dehumanize them so that they turn into subhuman species.

De-legitimization starts with the promotion of the forgery "The Protocols of the Elders of Zion" available in all good book shops in the Palestinian territories, blood libels and calls for boycotts are quick to follow. Hamas' blood libels appear in their crudest form in the Palestinian media for local consumption (two clicks away if you just search Google for anti-Semitic cartoons and videos put out by the PA) but for global consumption they orchestrate small "asymmetrical" wars. They lob a few thousand rockets at Israel until Israel is provoked to retaliate. Inevitably innocent little children are killed, and the western media are always conveniently at hand to broadcast these tragic images round the world. Very few Israelis die in these exchanges as they spend their lives underground in shelters during the hostilities. One questions why Hamas hasn't gone the same lengths to protect their own innocents underground when their own command structure, leadership and weapon stores are so well protected. At the end of these skirmishes the body count is unequal and the world calls foul, boo, unfair-100 to 1 against Gaza's population. Egged on by the pro-Palestinian lobby the decent liberal minded Guardian readers, who always support the underdog, start calling for boycotts. Playing underdog is a very valuable weapon in this war played out on the World Wide Web. In practice Hamas in Gaza and Hezbollah in Lebanon are supplied and armed by Iran and are handy clients for softening up the enemy whilst winning the sympathy of two thirds of the UN. Iran's unequivocal and oft-stated policy is to deny the last holocaust and promise the second. Hamas shares that global view. In our long history we Jews have learnt to trust our enemies, what they promise they try to deliver. So, step one of the process described in Yad Vashem is nearly complete with the delegitimization, demonization and boycotting of Israel.

These views are comfortably entrenched in the Arab and Muslim world but that's to be expected what really alarms me is how these attitudes have now taken root in nice western liberal democracies like Sweden, Denmark, France, Greece, and Italy. In the UK the trade unionist movement, most of Scotland, most of the university student unions and the Guardian readership are on board. The Labor Party, when under the leadership of Jeremy Corbyn, equated Zionism to fascism and is antisemitic to the core.

Palestinian propaganda today is the echo of Nazi propaganda exemplified by *Der Stürmer* with cartoons of ugly stereotypical Jews counting money or drinking children's blood. Popular soap operas on the TV stations of the PA portray Jews capturing innocent

## Why I Am a Zionist?

children to drain their blood to prepare matzoth for Passover and again and again Jews depicted as rats and monkeys. If you don't believe me, it's only two clicks away on Google.

Of course, nice liberally minded well-educated Englishmen won't accept any of this crap, but they don't need to. The consequence of de-legitimization will mean that the liberal democracies of the civilized world will not see the destruction of Israel as their problem in fact they might even view it as a step towards global peace just like the Nazi occupation of the Sudetenland in Czechoslovakia in September 1938. Only afterwards will they express shock and disbelief. As it was in Nazi Germany, so it was in Rwanda and Srebrenica, but we won't let it happen by default in Israel although we do risk some unpopularity in the UN.

Anyway, enough of this doom and gloom let me lighten the tone and tell you something uplifting we saw on our visit to the north of Israel. About an hour's drive north of Tel Aviv on the coastal highway you turn east just before Haifa towards the vineyards of Zikron Yakov. From there if you turn southeast, you enter one of the most beautiful areas in this part of the world; the southern Galil. Along the way every hilltop is capped with a gleaming white Arab village or town. The villages each have a mosque and the towns each have two mosques with minarets competing for dominance. 20% of the population of Israel are Muslim and live safely in their towns and villages of the southern Galil by choice. They enjoy equal access to health care and education. The chief of oncology in the Ziv university hospital nearby Safad, is a personal friend name of Jamal Zidan. He grew up in a Druze village not too far away. Another of our friends is Ishmael Khaldi; he grew up as a Bedouin shepherd boy in the Carmel hills just north of Zikron Yakov, a bright lad, did well at the local school and went on to study law and politics at Haifa university. He was once on the diplomatic staff at the Israeli embassy in London. Although a Muslim he joined us for Friday night dinner when my wife lights the Sabbath candles.

## Why Am I a Jew?

In contrast Gaza is completely *judenrhein* and when, as we both hope, there is a two-state solution, it is unlikely that Jews and their houses of worship would be tolerated.

Carrying on towards the Sea of Galilee about 25Km east of Mount Tabor, topped off with the basilica of the transfiguration of Christ, you reach the "River Jordan Village".

The village is set in beautiful grounds with gardens, stables, a children's zoo and a vertiginous adventure playground with rock climbing, abseiling and bungee jumping for children of all ages and abilities including those confined to wheelchairs. The same applies to a gigantic swimming facility with direct wheelchair access. By now it should be obvious that this village is in fact a holiday camp for chronically ill or severely handicapped children. We were shown round the facilities by the chairman of the project, Chaim Topol of "fiddler on the roof" fame, who explained how the camp provided respite for the parents and holidays for severely dependent children with a team of volunteer doctors, nurses, and councilors at hand round the clock. They could just about cope with 96 sick kids at a time and the group who were just ending their vacation as we visited, where insulin dependent diabetics whose blood sugar and insulin dosage needed constant monitoring.

The demography of the sick kids matched the demography of Israel as far as race and religion is concerned. What might surprise you though is that over the last 12 months 40 children from Gaza have also enjoyed a week at this holiday camp free of charge. All these children have chronic disabling conditions and when not on holiday in the southern Galil are cared for by the Israeli health care system although to be fair it can be difficult and humiliating for them and their parents to stand in line at check points to get to their out-patient appointments on time. Of course, things might be eased for them if they hadn't voted in a government with the political platform for the total annihilation of Israel and the Jewish people. You and I experience something similar as we stand in line to get through airport security holding up our trousers because our belts have been confiscated just in case we might be Islamic Jihad freedom fighters.

## Why I Am a Zionist?

It goes without saying, the good news about Israel and its treatment of its Arab citizens makes no news in the leftist liberal British press. The accepted narratives just focus on the lies of "asymmetrical wars", "ethnic cleansing" and "apartheid", so you'll just have to come to see things for yourself. Such a visit may help you in your laudable search for a balanced point of view.
Best wishes from your old classmate,
*Mike*

# Chapter 10

## *The God of Inner Space*

*To see a world in a grain of sand*
*And a heaven in a wildflower*
*Hold infinity in the palm of your hand*
*An eternity in an hour.*
WILLIAM BLAKE

IN THIS CHAPTER, I will suggest the role that religion *should* play in our increasingly secular world. To begin with I would like to quote from an invited lecture I delivered at an international conference, "The Role of the Learned Societies in Improving the Quality of Life in the Context of Globalization" in Bangkok, Thailand in June 2012.

> *Thou shalt love thy neighbor as thyself.* Leviticus 19:18
>
> *I choose to start my presentation by recalling the Old Testament commandment shown above, to remind us of all that whatever race, religion, or culture we come from, the simple command to love one's neighbor as ourselves, is the*

*bedrock of civilization. In response to this command, we should ask ourselves two simple questions, a) how do we best express our love? And b) who do we consider to be our neighbor? If one loves oneself then what is your single most important gift you would grant yourself? Ask anyone this question and they most always reply, the gift of good health. Therefore, if you love others then the gift you want for them is also good health. These others who you should love in an unconditional way are your parents, your spouse, your children, and grandchildren. I have 9 of the last category, and these are the easiest to love unconditionally. I might then go on to joke that I hate my neighbors, that that is of course taking the words of the bible too literally. To whom does this duty or commandment to love to extend? How wide is this circle of love? The immediate family, the extended family, our village, our tribe, or our Nation state? The answer to this is simple and contained within the very title of this symposium. With globalization of commerce, social network information technology and relative ease of travel, the concept of the global village has matured and with this the duty of care from those countries that are resource rich to those countries that are resource poor, becomes an ethical imperative. If we love our neighbors as ourselves, then we cannot stand by and watch them suffer nor must we squander scarce resources for tiny incremental improvements in health care for the rich whilst the poor of this world die prematurely from easily preventable or treatable disease.*

There are only two meaningful outcome measures in the evaluation of health care simply put; they are length of life (LOL) and quality of life (QOL). All other outcomes are surrogate and however compelling the results screening, blood tests and medical images might be, they may not translate into improvements in LOL and QOL. LOL is of course easy to measure but even cancer "survival" statistics can be misleading unless they translate into mortality reduction. QOL is not that easy to measure but psychometric instruments for this purpose have been available since the mid 1970s and are constantly refined and validated.

## MEASURING QOL

My mother, Mary, died on May 31st, 1974, which coincided with my 37th birthday. She had been suffering from advanced breast cancer and agonizing pains from skeletal metastases, for 12 months. Her doctors falsely believed that adequate pain relief with morphine might shorten her life and as my parents were very orthodox, they were reluctant to increase the dose of morphine. To make matters worse she was treated with a hideous cocktail of cytotoxic drugs that achieved nothing other than the loss of her long lustrous black hair. They were living in London at the time whilst I was working as a senior lecturer in the department of surgery at the University of Wales teaching hospital in Cardiff. I felt a mixture of anger, guilt and shame, for not intervening at the time. I promised myself redemption if at least I did my very best to make sure that none of my patients in the future would be allowed to die in this way. I realize that in writing that last sentence I'm painting myself in a good light, yet the shame I feel for not having the courage of conviction to argue with my mother's medical attendants, lives with me to this day.

As chance would have it, I had set up a special clinic at the radiotherapy center in Velindre, just North of Cardiff, to manage the care of women with advanced breast cancer. I shared this clinic with a young medical oncologist, Dr Terry Priestman. The drug we now call Tamoxifen, but then known by a number, ICI46,474, had just become available for the treatment of women in our clinic. We thought the best way of evaluating it was in a randomized controlled trial comparing the new "anti-estrogen" with the latest combination of cytotoxic drugs, VPCMF (Vincristine, Prednisone, Cyclophosphamide, Methotrexate and 5 Fluorouracil). Because tamoxifen had very little in the way of side effects and VPCMF was the poisonous mixture my mother had suffered, we thought we should measure and compare toxicity and well-being at the same time (QOL). Although an obvious thing to do with the benefit of hindsight, no instrument for measuring QOL existed at the time. So, we had to invent one. When cogitating on this I came across an advert for a brand of aspirin that advocated the use of the drug for when you felt "one degree under". Well-being measured in degrees—what a great idea. Instead of measuring the degrees on a thermometer we thought we would measure these subjective outcomes in centimeters along a 10-cm line with each end of the line marked by extremes. For example, the summary measurement for "well-being" was marked "never felt worse" at one end and "never felt better" at the other end. The patient then made an arbitrary mark at some point along the line. We would then measure the distance along the line from the "never felt worse" extreme and then allocate a score in cm.

10 cm would be "never felt better" whilst say 7.0 cm is how I feel now after a disturbed night of sleep haunted by nightmares. This we learnt, was a Linear Self-Assessment (LASA) that had been used in market research to test brand satisfaction but had never been applied in medical care. We then went on to develop the tool to cover 25 domains of subjective status. These were broadly divided up into physical symptoms, such as pain, nausea and vomiting and psychological symptoms such as anxiety, depression, and insomnia.

When tested on a pilot group we quickly noted that the scores for individual patients were consistent on a daily basis over a two-week trial although you couldn't make cross comparisons within the group because of wide variations. We then decided that the exact measurement on any day was not important but the trend for better or worse scores would count as our outcome measure. We published the method in the Lancet in 1976, and then published our first analysis of the trial comparing chemotherapy with tamoxifen in the British Medical Journal (BMJ) two years later. These data demonstrated that there was a greater objective response rate in the chemotherapy group but as might be expected the QOL scores were better in the tamoxifen group. A bizarre observation, that was almost metaphysical in its explanation, was that the QOL scores started to fall in advance of objective evidence of treatment failure. Despite the more dramatic objective responses in the chemotherapy group, when it came to survival there was no significance between the two arms of the study. Others went on replicate our findings but medical oncologists to this day, are more impressed with the rate of early objective shrinkage of the cancer deposits than the more important outcome of overall survival once symptom control has been achieved.

Leaving that behind, let's return to the measurement of QOL. The LASA technique was adopted for a while but found to be clunky and awkward to administer. Many patients couldn't grasp the concept and preferred to write an answer along the 10cm line. The mathematical analysis was complex as patients tended to prefer to concentrate their marks at one extreme or another. Since then, a whole industry has emerged of better and fully validated psycho-metric instruments, and we now have an international organization (ISOQOL) to promote and research this aspect of medical practice. As an example, a very popular tool, the EORTC QLQ-C30, that assesses the quality of life of cancer patients. It has been translated and validated into 81 languages and is used in more than 3,000 studies worldwide. Various modules have been developed for disease specific treatment measurements. These days, most major randomized controlled trials of cancer therapy, would not be funded unless there was a QOL module described in the protocol submitted for funding. These data are then incorporated into health economic considerations in organizations like NICE (National Institute of Clinical Excellence) using the measure described as a QALY (quality adjusted life years), that incorporate QOL and LOL into a single unit. Some new drugs are judged unaffordable if the cost is more than £30,000 a QALY. Of course, you can't put a value on a patient's life but here you have a clash of categorical imperatives, beneficence versus distributive justice.

More recently new psychometric instruments have been developed that include "spirituality" in the equation. One of these new tools, developed by Lynn Underwood in the USA, is called the Daily Spiritual Experience Scale (DSES). It is a 16-item self-report measure designed to assess ordinary experiences of connection with the transcendent in daily life. It includes constructs such as awe, gratitude, mercy, sense of connection with the transcendent

## The God of Inner Space

and compassionate love. Low scores in these domains are co-expressed with clinical anxiety and depression. It is becoming increasingly accepted as judged by the number of citations, but I have no experience in its use. The point I'm trying to make here, quoting the words of Lord Kelvin, who described the first and second laws of thermodynamics. "To measure is to know. If you cannot measure it, you cannot improve it."

At this point I want to turn my attention to the practice of religion. I feel strongly, that if religion is to grow and prosper, it must take a good look at itself and try and emulate or complement the aims and objective of the practice of good medicine, *to improve the length and quality of life* amongst their flock. That is the true expression of the edict in Leviticus, *thou shalt love thy neighbor as thyself,* as I expounded in the opening paragraphs of this chapter. These days, responsible physicians, do their best to practice evidence-based medicine (EBM), why should religion have a privileged role in our society? Surely there should be such a thing as evidence-based religion (EBR)? I must emphasize that I'm not talking about demanding proof for miracles such as burning bushes or virgin births, I am simply applying the guidelines of our advertising standards authority (ASA). It's one thing for an Irish brewery to have a poster campaign featuring a toucan, claiming "Guinness is Good for You, just see what toucan do", but is it acceptable to have posters outside churches or on double-decker buses that claim, "Religion is Good for You!"? Let us now consider EBR and judge whether the Churches, Mosques and Synagogues can do a little better. We have no duty of respect for these organizations unless they demonstrate that they can live up to our expectations as promoted by their pious words. The history of mankind has been littered with false prophets.

## DOES RELIGION IMPROVE LENGTH OF LIFE?

The answer to that rhetorical question is a resounding yes! Nor should we be surprised.

## Why Am I a Jew?

Leviticus is full of advice on public health, hygiene, and dietary advice. Given that these laws were written for the benefit of nomadic tribes living in the desert, many of those admonitions apply today. The foundation laws of *kashrut* that equally apply to *halal*, made sense in the Biblical era and during the rise of Islam in the 7 C in part because of the risk of tape worm from pigs and dysentery from microbes commonly found in shellfish or allergies to some proteins found in crustaceans. I learnt the hard way about my allergy to prawns when I had a coronary angiogram a few years back.

Over the millennia from Biblical times, religious authorities have warned about the hazards of substance abuse and promiscuous sex. A day of rest, whether it happens to be on Friday, Saturday, or Sunday, is a good idea for a healthy lifestyle. The odd fast day can do us no harm as with avoiding eating red meat on a Friday. And to reiterate, if you live in a community where others who share your concerns, you will not be left wanting. Another vignette to illustrates this point, goes back 10 years when my wife had major surgery for spinal stenosis. Her spinal cord was trapped by bony protrusions and degenerate discs at the level of C3/4 in the neck. She was at serious risk of becoming paraplegic. A brilliant act of surgery, that involved removing two cervical vertebrae and three discs and replacing them with prostheses, was completed with great success but my wife was not allowed to do anything energetic for a month to six weeks. I took time off work to care for her and in addition the community rallied round. I ended up nearly drowning in chicken soup. I can imagine that if my wife had been a widower, she would not have had to rely on the over-stretched social services, volunteers from the community care committee would have filled the gaps. So, I've explained why religion should improve LOL, but a scientist is never satisfied with a *should*. The sun should orbit the earth, but it doesn't and of greater importance to me; I should be rich but I'm not. I'm happy that in this case for once, my prejudices have been vindicated by evidence. A paper was published at the end of December 2017, in the highly regarded and peer reviewed journal, PLOS med., with the title, "Religion,

## The God of Inner Space

a social determinant of mortality? A 10-year follow-up of the Health and Retirement Study". The authors analyzed data gathered between 2004 and 2014 on more than 18,000 participants. They then applied statistical tests to calculate the link between religious attendance and all-cause mortality during the decade studied. The researchers included variables such as religious attendance, the importance of religion, and religious affiliation. Gender, race or ethnicity, education, and income were also considered as potential determinants of health. They sum up the findings as follows: *After adjustment for confounders, attendance at religious services had a dose-response relationship with mortality, such that respondents who attended frequently (i.e., at least once a week) had a 40% lower hazard of mortality compared with those who never attended.*

Does religion improve quality of life? The answer to this rhetorical question might be—*could do better*. Let me remind you of my list of the adverse aspects of religion from the section, *the good the bad and the ugly*: Belief in Heaven and hell, Teaching of sexual guilt, Denial of sexual orientation, Promotion of celibacy as a virtue, Anti-abortion and contraception and Misogyny. I've already explained my attitude to "Bad" aspects of religious faith from the viewpoint of moral philosophy but I want to look again at this list for the impact these attributes of religion have on the quality of life for the individual. Religious leaders are beholden to exhibit a degree of humility, accept that what they preach might do harm and do their best to improve the quality of life (QOL) of their congregation. Let's start with Heaven and Hell. You cannot legislate against such beliefs, but you can at least temper the way they impact on QOL. The clergy should teach that virtue is its own reward and that to be virtuous in this life for the benefit of life after death in 5-star accommodation, is not a virtue but merely succumbing to bribery and that is a sin. The same applies to the concept of hell. Avoiding the temptation to covet thy neighbor's wife so as not to spend an eternity in a furnace stoked by demons, is not a virtue, such behavior never ends up well in any case. Furthermore, throughout history there was never any evidence that preaching fire and brimstone reduced the crime rate. I would go a little further, that should a religious leader preach this despicable load of garbage in front of vulnerable children, he or she should be reported to the appropriate secular authorities. Celibacy is not a virtue but a punishment for a crime not committed.

> *And God blessed Noah and his sons and said to them, "Go forth, be fruitful and multiply, and fill the earth"*, Genesis 9:1

If you believe this is the word of God, then please note what God *didn't* say by way of a qualifying clause. There was no codicil to the effect that the act of multiplication should on no account be pleasurable punishable by an additional term in the sin bin. The very fact that sexual intercourse is one of the greatest joys of life, bettered only by a good run down a black run on the *piste* on a sunny day in the Alps, accounts for its evolutionary advantage. The caste of high priests around the world should cease and desist from threatening their flock with fire and brimstone should they find pleasure in "recreational" sex with a consenting partner. This doesn't mean that promiscuity is endorsed, such behavior carries its own penalty and should be included in the school curriculum as sex education.

The etiology of sexual orientation is complex and currently open to debate. Whether it's nature or nurture or a bit of each, has yet to be resolved, but all agree that it is out of one's control and therefore should no longer be considered as a crime for prosecution in secular courts or as a sin for prosecution in the heavenly courts. The suffering of millions of young men and women over the last 2,000 years can only be imagined. I have little doubt that the acceptance of the LGBT community in recent years has enhanced their QOL scores that must have been at the lowest extreme in the era dominated by religious bigots and bullies. Of course, there are many benighted countries in the world today who deal with the LGBT community by throwing them from a roof top. This way not only has their QOL been impaired, but their LOL has been shortened. This is murder and those guilty should be put on trial in some international court of justice.

## The God of Inner Space

Finally, I wish to consider the three issues, anti-abortion, contraception, and misogyny, under the same heading. By these means women are denied their rights of self-determination. Why should we continue to accept the right of elderly, celibate, bigoted men, to bully women of all ages in their fertile years and deny the women their right to determine when and how many times they should give birth. Again sex-education in schools should take on the role of advising against promiscuity and the hazards of young teen-age pregnancies. Let the clergy preach about the virtue of love, their role in determining the birth rate is long past. I am glad to note the increasing role of women in high office in the Church of England and in many of the "center left" Jewish communities around the world. Once female clergy balance male clergy in positions of authority in all religious communities, the problem would be solved but we still have a long way to go. I concede that many of my most provocative recommendations above will have angered religious leaders in the spectrum "center-right to extreme right wing" but I doubt they will have persisted so far into this book. Yet I am very sensitive to the fact that I might have offended many dear friends and family members who don't share my views. For them I offer a gamble, the flip side of Pascal's wager, because it excludes those who believe that this life on earth is merely a preparation for the life to come. Let us put our conflicting ideas to the test by conducting a trial or natural experiment. Let us take a large sample from our population that will include believers and non-believers. The believers would be stratified by their religious affiliations, and all stratified by demography (age, sex, country of birth, social class etc.) Let us then study this cohort by offering psychometric QOL instruments that include the DSES, and let the best man win. I will start off by testing myself on the DSES scale that, to remind you, covers spiritual domains such as awe, gratitude, mercy, sense of connection with the transcendent and compassionate love. The first thing to note about the DSES is the caveat at the top of the page that reads as follows: *Several items use the word "God". If this word is not a comfortable one for you, please substitute another word that calls to mind the divine or holy for you.*

# Why Am I a Jew?

There are 16 items on the scale that are scored from left to right, *many times a day, every day, most days, some days, once in a while, never.* I assume that the nearer your tick is to the left hand extreme the better the score (*Many times a day,* scores 6 and *never,* scores 1) Using this system I score 53 out of a possible 96. I got top marks for the following items: *I am spiritually touched by the beauty of creation, I feel thankful for my blessings, I feel a selfless caring for others, I accept others even when they do things, I think are wrong.* Of course, this is self-assessment, but I tried to be honest with myself otherwise I would have done better than a measly 55%.

# Chapter 11

## *Baruch Spinoza I*

THE FIRST RABBI IN HISTORY to be excommunicated for heresy that I've been able to discover, was Elisha ben Abuja, a member of the Sanhedrin in the Greco-Roman period sometime after the debacle of the Bar Kochba rebellion in 132–135 C.E. Apparently, he was seduced by the rational thinking of classical Greek scholarship and culture. My source for this knowledge came by chance at a dinner party when I mentioned that I was working on a book that contained sections on Spinoza. A guest at this dinner recommended of book written by Milton Steinberg in 1939, entitled "As a driven Leaf". This excerpt sums up the story:

> His lasting fame-or infamy-rests on his having been one of the minute number of rabbis excommunicated during the eight hundred years of the Rabbinic period. The reason for the excommunication has come down to us in a tale. It appears that one day Elisha ben Abiah stood watching as a man climbed up a ladder to send away a mother bird before taking down its nest of fledglings, in conformity with the law in Deuteronomy, for the observance of which the Bible promises a long life (22:6,7). Instead, the man fell

> *to his death. Enraged and appalled by what he had witnessed, Elisha ben Abuja denied divine providence with the words: "There is no justice, and there is no judge." And was excommunicated.*

Elisha barely leaves a footprint in the sands of time, yet Spinoza's voice, through his writings, thunders down to us from mid 17thC Amsterdam. To me he was one of the greatest philosophers of all time and one of the leaders of the age of enlightenment. As I will show, his message is as relevant today as it was 350 years ago.

Baruch Spinoza was the son of Michael d'Espinoza an importer of dried fruit and nuts from the Iberian Peninsula. Michael was a well-respected member of the Amsterdam Jewish community and acted as a *parnas* (elder or representative) of the union of the three orthodox synagogues and a governor of the communities' schools. Baruch rapidly showed his affinity for study, logic, and dialectics before he reached the age of 14 when he left school to join his father's business. Although his formal education was over, he continued on his own volition to study the Torah and the Talmud. At a very early age he made known his "heretical" views during open discourse amongst adult study groups. Even before publishing his first works, he was already in trouble by advocating his opinion that the Torah was not of divine origin, that Moses should command no more respect that Mohammad or Jesus of Nazareth. He also expounded his views that there was no afterlife of the soul. Even though he was only a callow youth, perhaps trying to provoke controversy and attention seeking, the community went incandescent with rage and on the 27 of July 1656 pronounced a *herem* (excommunication) on the young man. I acknowledge the scholarship of Sir Simon Schama in providing the words of this decree.

> *By the decree of the Angels and by the command of the holy men, we excommunicate. Expel, curse and dam Baruch de Espinoza with the consent of God . . . cursed be he by day and cursed by he by night; cursed by he when he lies down and cursed by he when he rises up . . . . . The Lord shall not spare him and the Lord shall blot out his name from under*

# Baruch Spinoza I

> *heaven. . . . . .no one shall communicate with him in speech or writing nor accord him any favor nor stay under the same roof as him nor be within four cubits of his vicinity nor shall read any treatise composed or written by him.*

And that's just a shortened version! It is difficult to understand the fierceness and bile of this decree making an outcast of a naive young contrarian before he had published a word. His first work, *Treatise on the Emendation of the Intellect,* was written in about 1660, where he argues in favor of a worthwhile life rather than a pointless death. This beautiful line of prose in the Treatise reads to me as an adumbration of all that was to follow.

> *But love towards a thing eternal and infinite feeds the mind wholly with joy and is itself unmingled with any sadness wherefore it is greatly to be desired and sought after with all our strength.*

Eventually Spinoza selects to exile himself to a nearby village rather than living in the toxic environment anywhere near the Amsterdam Jewish community. There left in peace, he trained as a lens grinder and continued his studies and writings. It is something of a cliché to say that his lenses allowed him to see more clearly than his Jewish compatriots. It remains a mystery why this young man was subjected to a *herem* and such a vicious decree. Simon Schama argues eloquently that the Hebrew congregation in Amsterdam weren't as secure and as welcome in the gentile community as many think. He suggests that they were tolerated if they adhered to the teachings of the Old Testament that was part of the Christian heritage as much as that as the Jewish canon. Furthermore, as far as the Calvinist Dutch Reformed church were concerned, one was defined by their monotheistic religion. Therefore, there was no such thing as a "secular Jew", until Spinoza unintentionally, invented it. Yet he was not an atheist as I will argue below. The most famous secular Jew of all time was Albert Einstein. Einstein proudly claimed he was a Jew and when challenged to explain what kind of Jew he was, he replied, "I believe in Spinoza's god who reveals himself in the lawful harmony of the world, not in a God who concerns himself with the fate and doings of mankind."

Although as you shall soon see that Spinoza and I are on the same side, making sense of his original writings is a chore and much is simply beyond my understanding. I am therefore indebted to Sir Roger Scruton for helping me make sense of a philosopher who is central to the revolutionary ontological understanding of God at the time of the Enlightenment. (Ontology is a word favored by philosophers that is not in common use by normal folk like us. Ontology is the philosophy of the nature of being. An ontological argument in this context is the philosophical argument for the existence of God.)

In an attempt to understand Spinoza's ontological arguments for the existence of God, and not wanting to rely on tertiary sources, I buried myself into a translation of "The Ethics" kindly provided in paper-back format by Amazon. Perhaps drowned myself rather than buried myself would be more appropriate, as I had to keep coming up for air. I'm a bookworm, I've read avidly since the age of 7, I've read books on arcane molecular biology, and I've even read Popper's "Conjectures and refutations" but "The Ethics", although using the English translation, is unreadable. Nevertheless, after two or three attempts in a quiet room, in my most comfortable armchair and with a glass of the finest Talisker in easy reach, the penny dropped. Here was I in the 21stC, a disciple of Karl Popper, someone steeped in the scientific school of falsifiability and hypothetico-deductivist logic, trying to make sense of the philosophical writings of a 17thC Dutchman proving his propositions using Euclidian inductive logic and deductive syllogisms that were promoted by Aristotle. A syllogism is a form of reasoning in which a conclusion is drawn from two given or assumed propositions (premises); a common or middle term is present in the two premises and a conclusion. Here are two examples:

1. All men are mortal
   Socrates is a man
   *ergo*. Socrates is mortal.

2. Van Gogh was a great artist
   Van Gogh never sold a painting in his lifetime
   I'm an artist whose paintings never sell *ergo* I'm great.

My problem is aggravated by the fact that Spinoza uses words like "substance", "attributes" and "essence" that have different meanings in 17thC philosophy from what we would understand today. I also confess to having a problem with the words inductive and deductive. Essentially inductive logic makes predictions from repeated observation to a generalized conclusion whilst deduction assumes that if certain premises are true then the conclusions are true. It wasn't until the insights of the Scottish philosopher, David Hume (1711–1776), that these ancient Greek concepts of logic where overturned. Many of my readers who are familiar with the "Black Swan" phenomenon that is beautifully examined in Nassim Nicholas Taleb's book of the same name", will understand what I mean. Ultimately the logic favored by Spinoza was dismissed by Bertrand Russell's in his book "The History of Western Philosophy" (1945), when he goes so far as to say "Aristotelian logic was a dead end followed by 2,000 years of stagnation.... I conclude that the Aristotelian doctrines are wholly false, anyone in the present day who wishes to learn logic will be wasting his time."

Despite all that, what I find remarkable that when you leave out all the antiquated logic and just look at the conclusions for each test of the truth, he ends up pre-empting most of my deductions that emerge by applying modern scientific philosophy.

First is he an atheist? Well clearly no, as the first half of "The Ethics" sets out to prove the existence of God. He applies 37 propositions based on axioms (premises, truisms) and concludes that there is a God if defined in his precise way.

*"Whatever is; is in God, and nothing can exist or be conceived without God."*

So, what is beyond doubt is that Spinoza's achievement was to show man and his world as an inextricable unity, and man himself master and servant of the fate that creates him.

That reads very much like the first three principles of faith of Maimonides. Spinoza also agrees with Maimonides that numbering items is a human construct, and as you can't use anthropomorphic concepts to describe the attributes of God even his "oneness" is somewhat heretical. Spinoza defines God as a "substance consisting of infinite attributes, each of which expresses eternal and infinite essence." Translated into more familiar terms, God is not distinct from the world but identical with it. *Deus sive Natura*-God or Nature.

In the appendix to this section, he concludes.

> *In the foregoing I have explained the nature and properties of God. I have shown that he necessarily exists, that he is one: that all things are in God, and so depend on him, that without him they could neither exist nor be conceived."*

From this bedrock, following many steps of Aristotelian logic that I cannot follow, Spinoza arrives at a definition of good and bad behavior.

> "By good, I understand that which we certainly know to be useful to us; by bad, I understand that which we certainly know will prevent us from partaking of any good. The good life is that which is most favorable to our nature, the bad life which it is most opposed. Vice and wickedness are to be avoided, not because they are punished by God (who engages in no such absurd endeavors), but they are at variance with our nature and lead us to despair."

His concept of virtue described in section 4 proposition XXXVI, follows on from this and serves as a practical guide to the way we should conduct our lives.

> *The highest good of those who follow virtue is common to all and therefore all can rejoice therein. To act virtuously is to act in obedience with reason, and whatsoever we endeavor to do in obedience to reason is to understand the highest good for those who follow after virtue is to know God.*

Well, he gets there in the end with his ontological discourse: virtue, verily is its own reward.

In the sections where he explores our emotions, he concludes with several aphorisms concerning love and other emotions that I find refreshing. Some examples:

> "Hatred is increased by being reciprocated, and on the other hand can be destroyed by love. Hatred which is completely vanquished by love passes into love: and love is thereupon greater if hatred had not preceded it."
>
> "Pity is pain accompanied by the idea of evil which has befallen someone else to be like ourselves. Benevolence is the desire of benefitting one whom we pity".

Finally, what must have appeared outrageous to the Rabbinate at the time, was this assertion:

> "The conceptions of wrath, punishment, reward, and compassion have no application to God, and it is a mistake to believe that God can be moved by our prayers or interested in fulfilling them"

Scientific philosophy has moved on a lot since then as I've already demonstrated, yet you will learn by the time you reach the end of this book, that I come to the same conclusions as Spinoza using modern epistemology. The only difference is that Spinoza finds God in infinite space whilst I find God closer to home.

# Chapter 12

## *Spinoza II: A Book Forged in Hell*

Is it heresy today to claim that you admire the teachings of Baruch Spinoza? I think not because others got there first. I wish to quote from a very interesting essay published by Dr Harris Bor in The Jewish Chronicle on 16 January 2017. Bor is a barrister who used to teach at the London School of Jewish Studies (LSJS).

> It might sound seem shocking to many that I teach the philosophy of Spinoza at LSJS, after all, he sought to replace the personal God of the Bible with the impersonal God of Nature. He saw the Bible as the work of man, Judaism as parochial, free will as an illusion and reason (rather than revelation) as the source of truth and path to salvation. It is hard to imagine ideas that pose more of a challenge to contemporary Orthodoxy, yet there is a relevance and spiritual power to Spinoza that is difficult to ignore. His ideas, radical in his time and influential even today, shake us from our complacency and call on us to up our religious game.

The boundary between religion and politics has eroded in recent years, despite the consensus on the right to freedom of

## Spinoza II: A Book Forged in Hell

conscience and on the need for some sort of separation between church and state. One reason for this trend is that religions are making strong claims on people's allegiance, and universal religions make these claims on all people, rather than just a particular community. For example, Islam has traditionally held that all people owe obedience to Allah's will. Thus, it is probably inevitable that religious commitments will sometimes come into conflict with the demands of politics. But religious beliefs and practices also potentially support politics in many ways. There has also been a growing interest in minority groups and the political rights and entitlements they are due. In the USA this trend is seen at the extreme right wing of politics as exemplified by Trumpism taking root in the both the "Bible belt" and "Rust belt" in the southern states and land locked states of the mid-west. This expresses itself by mandating teaching "creationism" in schools and draconian anti-abortion laws. In May 2019 the state of Alabama decried that abortion in most cases, including pregnancy following rape, was prohibited with the threat of 99 years in prison for the abortionist. They even use the rhetoric of the holocaust to describe the loss of the fetuses after first trimester termination of pregnancies. Along with this marching in lock step, we see the rise of homophobia, white supremacy, racism, and the reappearance of the burning cross. This and the right to bear arms to kill thy neighbor, for reasons beyond my power of judgment, appeals to the mindsets of these religious bigots.

For example, this appeared in the Washington Post on the 22 of May 2019.

> *"The evangelical right has for decades been very loud, very well organized and very convincing in their argument that the GOP could not survive without them. The price for their loyalty was an absolutist stand on abortion. (Opposition to same-sex marriage used to be as well, but — given that same-sex marriage is so widely accepted and without a shred of data showing harm to children, an old bugaboo on the right —that's gotten cut out from their list of demands.) Trump's ability to mesmerize the evangelical right and their utter subservience to him have made evident*

## Why Am I a Jew?

> to anyone paying the least bit of attention to politics that principle matters a whole lot less than power to these people. And as with guns, creating one-issue voters increases their political leverage".

In this fetid environment, it should not surprise us to see the re-awakening of antisemitism.

On October 27, 2018, while Shabbat morning services were being held, a Pittsburgh synagogue, the Tree of Life Congregation in the Squirrel Hill neighborhood, was attacked by a gun man with an assault rifle. Eleven people were killed and seven were injured. We lived in that neighborhood in 1970/71 when I was working in the labs of the Presbyterian hospital and befriended members of that community.

Left wing politics is a more complex mélange. What started as a Marxist/Leninist "anti-capitalism" revolutionary movement, has accretions like barnacles on the hull of an old wooden ship. As a young boy I was steeped in the literature and propaganda of communism, as that was the default position in our household. During the war "Uncle" Joe (Stalin) was one of my heroes, standing up to the Nazi army at the battle of Stalingrad. I read books by Ilya Ehrenberg and Mikhail Sholokhov, without realizing how much of it was Soviet propaganda. In those days it was respectable to be sympathetic to the communist cause when you read about the wealth and power of a tiny elite and the crushing poverty of the proletariat, not just in Russia, but in the UK as well. But with maturity and the disclosure of the gulags and the famine that decimated the population, we young political activists became skeptical. We learnt to sing different words to the Communist anthem:

> *The People's flag is palest pink, it's not so red as people think.*

Yet to this day our Labor party finds common cause with the Marxist ideology of the governments of Cuba and Venezuela. All in the name of anti-imperialism. Their protest marches can be seen as virtue signaling and self-love. Yet their protests are no longer about the poverty of the working classes but linked to a new cause;

## Spinoza II: A Book Forged in Hell

"victim culture". Concerns, are the needs of minority groups who are distinguished by their religion, as opposed to ethnicity, gender, or wealth. The one minority group who have suffered most because of their religious beliefs, the Jews, have been dropped out of the league table of victimhood and rebranded as rich, *white*, imperialists, who have driven the colored natives out of their homeland of Palestine in the creation of the racist, apartheid state of Israel. Hatred of Israel has fueled antisemitism and so we come full cycle as the extreme right and the extreme left find common cause.

> *Nazis crashing the Detroit Pride parade urinating on the Israeli flag and queer Jewish women being blocked from joining the DC dyke march for displaying the star of David. At the intersection of extreme ideologies is the hatred and obsession with Jews.*
>
> Tweet by Zak Sawyer June 9, 2019

So, it can be judged that religion has an impact across the political spectrum; bigoted interpretation of the Christian Bible on the right-hand side, and the definition of religious victimhood on the left-hand side.

There is a strange difference in the cultures of the UK and the USA in this regard. No presidential candidate in the USA would claim to be an atheist and must be seen in the company of religious clerics along with their smiling children, in promotional material. Whereas British politicians "don't do God" and would be embarrassed to confess that they attend church regularly. A recent exception to that rule was prime minister Theresa May and looked what happened to her!

Nevertheless, there has been a sinister thread in exploiting the beliefs in a constituency to win favor and win votes even to the extent of a "back door" blasphemy law. This is all to do with an attempt to define "islamophobia" in such a way that a challenge to Sharia law or questioning the attitude to women amongst radical Islamic critics, might be defined as a criminal act. The proposed definition has been opposed by many Britons, including British

Muslims, who warn that it would effectively shield Islam from scrutiny and valid criticism.

> "We are concerned that allegations of Islamophobia will be, indeed already are being, used to effectively shield Islamic beliefs and even extremists from criticism, and that formalizing this definition will result in it being employed effectively as something of a backdoor blasphemy law." — Open letter signed by 40 British academics, writers and public officials to Home Secretary Sajid Javid.

As I rewrite this paragraph, we learn that the victorious Taliban have taken control of Afghanistan and have reassured us that women's rights will be protected according to the laws of Sharia. Will any of our leaders be prepared to challenge that *reassurance* for fear of being labeled Islamophobic?

For comparison, and in order to provide balance, I will argue that to challenge circumcision of Jewish boys at 8 days, or the halachic laws governing animal slaughter is not antisemitic (see chapter 9), even though in the past, it has been used as a weapon by undisputed anti-Semites. Criticism of religious beliefs and practices does not amount to racism.

❊ ❊ ❊

In 1670, Baruch Spinoza published his *Tractatus Theologio-Politicus (Theological-Political Treatise)* anonymously. He was one of the first to spell out the hazard of allowing the theologians (religious clerics) to have a say in the running of the state and urged the separation of the church and the state. Yet 350 years on, his concerns are if anything magnified, and our House of Lords has Bishops and Archbishops sitting there by right.

## A BOOK FORGED IN HELL

One might have thought that the Jewish community over-reacted to this young *yeshiva bocher* (student at a Jewish seminary) thoughts, with an excommunication, but it was nothing compared with the

## Spinoza II: A Book Forged in Hell

response of the Dutch Church and their loyal burghers. One of these God-fearing men when criticizing *Tractatus Theologio-Politicus,* wrote as follows, "This book ought to be buried forever in an eternal oblivion, this atheistic book is full of abominations 'a book forged in hell' written by the devil himself". "A book forged in hell", is the title of a wonderful volume written by one of the world's greatest authorities on Spinoza, Steven Nadler. I'm using his first paperback issue published in 2014 by Princeton University Press as the main source of my material.

When the Tractatus first hit the booksellers on the canals of Amsterdam in 1670, the clergy went mad. The Reformed Church immediately set up a committee to deal with this threat to the very core of their faith. The North Holland Synod sent out this decree:

> *These Synod of Amsterdam desires that this licentious book is especially the harmful and should be dealt with under the old grievances regarding the blasphemous books. The deputies have taken all the necessary steps against the book with the first council of the court and are awaiting the outcome, the Christian Synod heartily abominates this obscene book and gives its thanks to the Honourable gentleman for their offer to suppress this writing as much as they can. . . . . . . .*

His writings were indeed suppressed and even burnt as an adumbration of the Nazi era.

Nadler sums up the central message of the Treatise as follows: "Every-day billions of people devote a significant amount of time to worshiping an imaginary being. Exposing this anthropomorphized God—who commands, judges and governs—as an organized superstitious fiction." Here he is speaking for or paraphrasing Spinoza—but I have little doubt that he endorses these teachings.

I would now like to look at several Spinoza's strongly held opinions that will sit comfortably with a modern secular society without saying at this juncture that I endorse those teachings.

# Why Am I a Jew?

## Separation of Church and State:

> *Reason therefore must not be the handmaiden of theology or vice versa and religion oversteps its bounds when it tries to limit intellectual inquiry and the free.*

I shall elaborate on this at the end of this chapter by providing a contemporary example that illustrates the hazards of ignoring Spinoza's schoolings with lethal outcomes.

## Miracles

> Miracles understood as supernatural divine interventions are strictly speaking impossible. Moreover, if miracles did in fact occur, they would testify not to God's infinite and internal power but on the contrary, to his limitations and even impotence for systems that requires outside interventions must be a rather imperfect systems and thus will reflect the incapacities or lack of foresight of its creator.
>
> No event can occur to contravene nature which preserves an internal fix and immutable order nothing can happen in nature to contravene her own universal laws nor yet anything that is not in agreement with these laws or does not follow from them.

It's worth noting at this point that Maimonides does not include the belief in miracles among the 13 essential principles of the Jewish faith he also appears to throughout the guide, to maintain a belief in natural causal determinism.

## Superstition

> Those who have most to gain from the continuation of such superstitious practices therefore take great pains to stabilize them and give them permanence they do this primarily by exaggerating the importance of these activities and surrounding them with impressive and dignified ceremonies. Religion stands in no need of the trappings of

# Spinoza II: A Book Forged in Hell

superstition. On the contrary, its glory is diminished when it is embellished with such fancies.

## Prophesy

Spinoza notes that all prophecy in the Hebrew Bible occurs by way of words or images the prophets hear voices and behold flashes of light they confront talking animals and Angels bearing swords. Some even apprehend God in bodily form hence it was not a more perfect mind that was needed for the gift of prophecy but a livelier imaginative faculty.

## Who wrote the Torah?

Don't ask! By now you should be able to predict what Spinoza preached and I wouldn't want to embarrass myself and my observant readers by spelling it out. Let's just say he went a bit further than our late beloved Rabbi Louis Jacobs . *(vide supra)* In his defense though I would like to quote this passage from Nadler's book.

> In the guide of the perplexed Maimonides is concerned to combat the anthropomorphizing of God to which common people and even the learned are prone. An infinite eternal being cannot have anything in common with finite creatures, there can be no analogy drawn between human beings and God and nothing about the divine nature can be known by considering human nature. This is obviously true in the case of body and many chapters of the guide are devoted to dispelling the notion that God has any physical features, but Maimonides also believes that the true understanding of God such as we could obtain it, must exclude attributing to God features of human psychology as well anger jealousy envy and other mental states.

Finally, the most compelling chapters of Spinoza's *Treatise* relate to Faith, Reason and the State. This is where I feel personally involved as a scientist constantly searching for the truth about life threatening disease and cognizant of the nature of evidence and causality. Amongst the clergy of the Calvinistic Dutch Republic and even more so amongst the Catholic neighboring states, there was much resistance to the "dangerous innovations" in science and philosophy. They presumed to have a say not only on matters of godliness but also on matters of truth. To quote Nadler again:

> It is this notion that the limits of science and philosophy are to be determined by religious criteria and this specially by scriptures in sectarian interpreters, that is the central objective Spinoza's attack in the treatise misunderstanding of the nature of faith and its relationship to truth and reason.

As Spinoza puts it, "Philosophy is the pursuit of knowledge, Religious Faith is about obedience. The fundamental teaching of scripture is a moral one; love thy neighbor. This is a principle discoverable by reason alone". He goes further in chapter 14 of his book, where he enumerates the seven principles of faith that are necessary for obedience to God's law. Number V states: "That the worship of God and obedience to him consist only in justice and loving-kindness, or in love of one's neighbor." In my chapter describing Spinoza's "Ethics" above, I explore how scientific philosophy of the present day reaches the same conclusion.

I want to conclude this chapter by discussing a very recent and tragic event that occurred in Israel on the night of the 29/30 of April 2021. 100,000 Charedim had gathered on Mount Meron, in a three-acre compound surrounding the grave of Rabbi Shimon Bar Yochai, an ancient Jewish sage whose death is commemorated each year in a pilgrimage on the Jewish festival of Lag B'Omer. Something happened (at the time of writing there has not yet been an inquest), and hoards panicked in in their haste to escape down the slippery slope of the entrance to the enclave, 44 people were trampled to death and hundreds seriously wounded. The United Synagogue to which I belong, responded appropriately on their website.

> The news is devastating. We are heartbroken that a night of celebration could so quickly turn to a day of mourning. We share the pain of all the families who have lost a

## Spinoza II: A Book Forged in Hell

*loved one and pray that the injured recover. As the Chief Rabbi said this morning: "As we struggle to come to terms with the horrific scenes of tragedy in Meron, the worst peacetime loss of life in Israel's history, this is a moment to unite in grief and prayer. May the memory of those lost to us forever be a blessing and may the injured be granted a refuah shelemah, a speedy recovery."*

The next day we learnt more about how this tragedy played out. It appeared that on April 10, Aryeh Deri, the interior minister, and Amir Ohana, the public security minister, held a meeting and agreed that despite pandemic restrictions, there would be no limits on the size of the gathering. Deri is the leader of the ultra-Orthodox party Shas, the second largest in the coalition and Ohana is a rising star in Netanyahu's Likud party and one of his closest lieutenants. Both ministers also attended the pilgrimage and Ohana was filmed, together with the police commanders, watching the crowds just hours before disaster struck on Friday. The health ministry had recommended that the number be limited to 10,000 this year, but that was, however, overruled by the two ministers. The relatives of the victims have not called for such an inquiry so far. "We are believers, and we don't seek for anyone to be guilty," said Avigdor Hayut, a teacher from Jerusalem, who lost Yedidya, his 13-year-old son, in the stampede. "We believe that everything God does is for a reason and now the important thing is to unite." Here we witness two fundamental principles defined in a book by an excommunicated heretic 350 years ago played out in front of eyes in the 21 Century in Israel, the Promised Land.

1. The "Church" not being separated from politics.
2. Suggesting that the tragedy was the will of God instead of the criminal negligence of man.

Compare this with the Hillsborough disaster, a fatal human crush during a football match at Hillsborough Stadium in Sheffield, South Yorkshire, England, on 15 April 1989. 94 young football supporters were crushed to death because of overcrowding in the central pens of the stand. There have already been two enquiries to establish cause and culpability by the secular courts and those guilty have paid the cost.

I think this is enough to vindicate Spinoza and to posthumously to rescind his excommunication.

# Chapter 13

## Faith in Science

IN THIS PENULTIMATE CHAPTER I want to revisit the apparent binary choice between faith or science. In Jonathan Sacks' masterly book. "The Great Partnership: God, Science and the Search for Meaning", he explores how religion has always played a valuable part in human culture and must be allowed to temper scientific understanding to fulfil our potential on this planet. He illustrates how scientific thinking is embedded deeply even in our religious understanding and is essential if we are to avoid the natural tendency for science to rule our lives rather than fulfilling its promise to set us free. He provides many quotes as illustrations of the case he is advocating amongst which is that of Tom Stoppard my favorite playwright.

> *"When we have found all the mysteries and lost all the meaning, we will be alone on an empty shore"*

In 2010 I published my memoires, "Breast Beating: A Personal Odyssey in the Quest for an understanding of Breast Cancer, the Meaning of Life and other easy questions." (Anshan Pub. Leighton

# Why Am I a Jew?

Buzzard). My conclusions regarding the meaning of life were as follows:

> There are of course, some mystical Chasidic sects who wish to explore the meaning of life and speculate on the afterlife, but mainstream Judaism accepts life as an end in itself and our religious teachings are primarily aimed at providing a code of conduct with more attention being paid to the relationships between man and man than between man and his God. Even to question whether life has a meaning may be a meaningless question to a Jew. If life is an end in itself then to question its meaning is as empty an exercise as to question the meaning of virtue, truth and beauty. If there is a meaning to life, then it has to be beyond our comprehension however many subtle clues may pass across our consciousness. We are analogous to the fish trying to comprehend life on earth when all its fish-like brain can perceive are distorted two-dimensional images that appear in its firmament. I would even go further and suggest it is the ultimate in intellectual arrogance to "know" the answer to this question. I happen to note that there is a tendency amongst those who "know" with certainty, to impose their beliefs on others and this in my opinion is the source of most of the world's problems. This confident knowledge of the unknowable leads to religious fundamentalism, forced conversion, terrorism and the three horsemen of the apocalypse.

Along with that, I included two of favorite quotations that illustrate the extremes of emotions when attempting to express one's outlook on the meaning of life. The first is the famous soliloquy from Macbeth Act V Scene V.

> "Tomorrow and tomorrow and tomorrow creeps in this petty pace from day to day to the last syllable of recorded time and all our yesterdays have lighted fools the way to dusty death. Out, out brief candle! Life's but a walking shadow. A poor player that struts and frets his hour upon the stage until he is heard no more. It is a tale told by an idiot full of sound and fury signifying nothing."

Macbeth Act V Scene V.

## Faith in Science

The second comes from George Bernard Shaw's book of prefaces.

> "This is the true joy in life, the being used for a purpose recognized by yourself as a mighty one, the being a force of nature instead of a feverish little clod of ailments and grievances complaining that the world will not devote itself to making you happy. I am of the opinion that my life belongs to the whole community, and as long as I live it is my privilege to do for it whatever I can. I want to be thoroughly used up when I die, for the harder I work the more I live. I rejoice in life for its own sake. Life is no brief candle to me. It is a sort of splendid torch which I have got hold of for the moment and I want to make it burn as brightly as possible before handing it on to future generations."

All the above make use of poetical metaphors describing the never-ending search for the meaning of life; alone on a lonely shore, fishes looking at the pond's surface, a guttering candle or a splendid torch. Yet however powerful and passionate the words they are still only metaphors. Is it true that without faith or a life without meaning, we fall into a slew of despair? Might there be evidence that loss of a meaning to our existence is linked to an early death or suicide?

In previous chapters I've described observational studies that suggest belonging to a faith community is associated with health gains and even increase in longevity. But these are not randomized clinical trials; association does not prove causality. Perhaps those who elect to become part of a religious community have already adopted healthy lifestyles. Maybe they love the countryside and long walks in fresh air? Maybe they tend to be non-smokers and enjoy a search for the sublime via literature, art and music? It then occurred to me that I'm familiar with a community where there is no choice. They are born into the community, and it is very rare for them to escape its clutches. I am of course thinking of the Charedi Jews again.

I recently began to take a more tolerant view of this sect after having watched the three series of the Netflix programmed, Tshtisel. My wife and I adored it and were crestfallen at the end.

(I do have it on the highest authority, that there will be a fourth series). Everyone I knew loved it as well and we were all at a loss to explain why we were so captivated. That aside, I suddenly realized that here was a perfect "natural experiment". Let us take a closed community in Jerusalem, living according to strict rules surrounded by a mixed population of all degrees of religiosity from the orthodox to the secular, of many different cultures and many different countries of origin, and compare their longevity.

Coming back to the TV series, one thing we can all agree on, they did not live "healthy" lives. They smoked, the men were fat, they took no exercise, ate a very unhealthy diet rich in fat and carbohydrate and were constantly short of money. All the older men in their kaftans and their unkempt beards, looked like walking examples of heart attacks about to happen. So, in real life, what is the expectation of life amongst Charedi men and women?

So, to refute the teachings of the Bible I made a deep search to see if the Charedi lifestyle was so unhealthy as to lead to a significant reduction in expectation of life.

The first detailed report I encountered was an item in Ynet News 2015.

> Report: Ultra-Orthodox in Israel healthier, live longer
>
> *Residents of cities that have a high concentration of ultra-Orthodox Jews have a much higher life expectancy than expected based on their socioeconomic status, the Taub Institute's annual report showed on Wednesday. The report showed that the vast majority, 73.6 percent, of ultra-Orthodox people defined their health as "very good", compared to 50 percent among other population segments. Furthermore, 18.7 percent of ultra-Orthodox Jews reported suffering from health problems—compared to double or more that rate among other populations. Researchers suggest that ultra-Orthodox people have relatively high social capital, which manifests in a proliferation of friendships, high satisfaction from family relationships, a supportive social system, and community volunteer work.*

## Faith in Science

> The report found that the average life expectancy among ultra-Orthodox men was about three years higher than would be expected based on their socioeconomic status. For women, life expectancy was two-and-a-half years higher than expected.

That was not what I was looking for and these findings can be dismissed as "ascertainment bias".

I speculated that these observations were "cherry picked" and also related to social norms among the ultra-Orthodox, who do not encourage complaining, especially in a national poll. At the same time, as a scientist of impeccable integrity, I had to consider the possibility that I was guilty of "confirmation bias." So, I made a deeper search and found this in the report from the Israeli Central Bureau of Statistics, 2012.

> *Long-Range Population Projections for Israel:*
>
> Haredi life expectancy is the same as for other Israeli Jews, and is projected to rise in similar fashion (from 80.8 years for men and 84.8 years for women in 2014 to 84.5 years for men and 89.3 years for women in 2034)

In this report there was no correction for socio-economic status but as if to rub salt into my wounds, here is what the Israeli National Insurance Institute discovered in their Poverty report in 2014.

> Poverty rates have been increasing since 2000. In 2013, 66.1% of Haredi families lived below the poverty line

To my amazement, I end up concluding that "social capital" carries the same value as financial capital in predicting life expectancy in the same way that social deprivation is a powerful predictive factor for longevity in the UK. That applies to all-cause mortality but let us take a closer look at suicide. I've just finished the novel "Machines like me" by Ian McEwan (Jonathan Cape, London 2019). This book explores the meaning of "mind" and sense of self by imagining an age when artificial intelligence (AI) allows for the building of robots who not only behave like humans but with greater and greater familiarity with their owners begin to think like humans and outperform them. In this work of fiction, the majority of the robots world-wide "commit suicide" by allowing their energy banks to run dry after they become sophisticated enough to realize they have no meaning in their artificial life. That of course is fiction but what is the evidence in reality? The first piece of evidence to support this conjecture was in a paper entitled, "Religiosity, Meaning in Life and Suicidal Tendency Among Jews".

These were their conclusions:

> "A significant and negative correlation was found between a sense of meaning in life and suicidal tendencies, beyond gender or level of religiosity. In addition, no difference was found in level of suicidal tendency between Jewish religious and Jewish secular youth; however, among Jewish religious teens, a lower level of depression was reported in comparison with their secular peers. The study therefore concludes that meaning in life is the dominant variable in minimizing suicidal tendencies among youth. The results of this study may promote the establishment of prevention, intervention and therapy plans, especially in the age range that is crucial for suicide. Such programs should be based upon finding meaning in life."

Identical findings were described within a population of South African University students. That alone might not convince you and I confess to a degree of skepticism as both papers were published in the journal of Religious Health, that might suggest a "publication bias". By this I mean that the editors prefer positive results and reject studies with negative outcomes. But then, as if by Divine intervention, the very next issue of the Journal of the American Medical Association (JAMA) carried a paper from the Health Retirement Study (HRS) with the title; "Association Between Life Purpose and Mortality Among US Adults Older Than 50 Years" The HRS is a national cohort study of American adults older than 50 years. The members of this cohort were between the ages of 51 to 61 and their spouses or partners who were enrolled regardless of age. Initially, individuals born between 1931 and 1941 were enrolled starting in 1992. The present prospective cohort study sample were those from 8419 HRS participants who were older than 50 years and who had filled out a psychological questionnaire during the HRS 2006 interview period. The final sample for analysis was 6985 individuals.

The "purpose in life" was assessed for the 2006 interview period with a 7-item questionnaire from the Ryff and Keyes Scales of Psychological Well-being. Evaluation using this scale ranged from 1 to 6, with higher scores indicating greater purpose in life. The primary outcome measures were for all-cause and cause-specific mortality analyses. Life purpose was significantly associated with all-cause mortality in the HRS comparing those in the lowest life purpose category with those in the highest life purpose category. Some significant cause-specific mortality associations with life purpose were also observed including cardiac, circulatory, and blood conditions; concluding that stronger "purpose in life" was associated with decreased mortality. From all of the above we can deduce that belief in a meaning of one's life, "Purposeful living", must have health benefits even though this is a metaphysical construct.

So, if we assume that the choice is binary, then we either must put our faith in faith or put our faith in science. The former relies on intuitions concerning untestable hypotheses whilst the latter relies on evidence from tested hypotheses. This cannot be true, so I needed to come up with a word that describes my world view of the faith/science nexus and then try and persuade you how it came about.

I found it difficult track down a word that fits the bill. I tried *equipoise*, but that simply means they weigh equally on the scales. I then tried *complementary*, but that word has already been hijacked to mean alternative (quack) medicine. Finally, I chose synergism, a word defined in the Oxford English dictionary as; *"the interaction or cooperation of two or more organizations, substances, or other agents to produce a combined effect greater than the sum of their separate effects"*.

## Why Am I a Jew?

The question can now be worded, is there an evolutionary advantage for synergism between faith and science and if so, is homo sapiens still evolving?

Early *Homo sapiens* emerged in the middle Paleolithic period roughly 300,000 years ago and it is taught that our species *developed* full behavioral modernity, roughly 50,000 years ago, corresponding to the start of the Upper Paleolithic period. In contrast the emergence of *"homo rationabilis"* can be dated to the age of enlightenment about 350 years ago!

> *Let us apply to the political and moral sciences the method founded in observation and calculation the method that is served us well in the natural sciences*
>
> Laplace a philosophical essay on probabilities 1806

I picked up that quotation from Ian Stewart's splendid and appropriately named book, "Do Dice Play God, The Mathematics of Uncertainty", Google Books, 2019, in which he describes the application of statistical reasoning to human attributes and behavior. From the time of Isaac Newton in the mid 18thC, science started making big advances and many scholars and philosophers were starting to argue that evidence-based science was superior to faith as a way to understand the natural world. The place of Christian beliefs previously considered to be absolute truths that virtue of the authority of God, were being usurped by mathematics. One of the first battles between the mathematics and scientific rationalism and the religious authorities, was led by Bishop Berkeley an Irish philosopher who developed a theory he called "immaterialism", later referred to as "subjective idealism" by others. This theory denies the existence of material substance and instead contends that familiar objects like tables and chairs are only ideas in the minds of perceivers and, as a result, cannot exist without being perceived. In other words, Berkley was trying to reverse Newton's ideas of space, time and motion. It is interesting to note that the Rev Thomas Bayes, another cleric, defended Newton against the accusations of the Bishop Berkeley. Bayes remains famous to this

## Faith in Science

day for another way of describing conditional probabilities using a statistical method we now describe as Bayesian methodology.

Of course, the most famous of all the battles between science and religiosity was the stand-off between Darwinian evolution and creationism. This became known as the Huxley-Wilberforce debate. The 1860 the British Society for the Advancement of Science organized a debate that took place at the Oxford University Museum in Oxford, England, on 30 June 1860, seven months after the publication of Charles Darwin's *On the Origin of Species*. Several prominent British scientists and philosophers participated, including Thomas Henry Huxley, Bishop Samuel Wilberforce, Benjamin Brodie and Joseph Dalton Hooker. The debate is best remembered today for a heated exchange in which Wilberforce supposedly asked Huxley whether it was through his grandfather or his grandmother that he claimed his descent from a monkey. Huxley is said to have replied that he would not be ashamed to have a monkey for his ancestor, but he would be ashamed to be connected with a man who used his great gifts to obscure the truth.

The other famous *cause celebre* took place in a courthouse rather than a university in Dayton Tennessee, USA in 1925. The case was listed as, The State of Tennessee v. John Thomas Scopes, better remembered as the "Monkey Trial". The State Representative was John W. Butler, a Tennessee farmer and head of the World Christian Fundamentals Association, who lobbied state legislatures to pass anti-evolution laws. The man summoned to defend the teaching of evolutionary theory was 24-year-old John T. Scopes, a Dayton high school science and math teacher. I remember vividly watching the play "Inherit the Wind" directed by Kevin Spacey, at the Old Vic, London in 2009. The theatre's artistic director also played Henry Drummond; an American lawyer who seeks to defend a teacher accused of breaking state law by teaching evolution to his students. This sense of righteous indignation I felt watching the drama play out was equivalent to that when I was in the audience for a performance of Brecht's Galileo.

For most of the resource wealthy and liberal Nations of the world today, the debate is over although it still festers away in some backward States of the USA today, where creationism endorsed by evangelical Christians. These States are also guilty of criminalizing women who seek abortion after rape.

As for me?—I see myself as continuing this journey of enquiry, led by the giants of science upon whose shoulders I ride, in the quest to reconcile the differences between faith and science. If left to nature, there would be a point in time where Faith and Science would ultimately reach a degree of synergism, as evolutionary pressure would see *homo sapiens* gradually superseded by *"homo rationabilis"*. Sadly, I don't see this happening in my lifetime or the lifetime of my children, as those with fixed religious beliefs that date back to Mediaeval thinking, have access to the weapons of mass destruction themselves one of the ugly consequences of the power of science.

# Chapter 14

## *My Search for the Divine*

*"Beliefs expressed in stories, objects, images and rituals unite believers, decrease anxieties and promote the formation of strong social bonds that help to make our worlds well-ordered and understandable. This starts with the human mind."*

JILL COOK, EXHIBITION CURATOR
OF LIVING WITH GODS, BRITISH MUSEUM 2017

THAT QUOTATION APPEARS IN the introduction to the catalogue for the wonderful exhibition at the British Museum that was running in London when I started writing this book. Everything starts with the human mind. It's like the philosophical conundrum: *if a tree falls in a forest remote from human habitation, does it make a noise?* My answer is, No. By noise we mean vibrations of the ear drum transmitted from a perturbation of the atmosphere and transported along the auditory nerves to the cerebral cortex. No receiver no signal. Religious belief starts with the human mind but what is the signal and where within the cranium does the mind exist?

## Why Am I a Jew?

I've already explained why I can't answer the question: "Are you an atheist?" Even worse is the assertion: "You can't be an atheist; you must be an agnostic". The Oxford English dictionary defines agnostic as; *a person who believes that nothing is known or can be known of the existence or nature of God.* That's absurd because it pre-supposes I know what "God" means in the first place. For example, can any of you reading this, believe that nothing is known or can be known about the existence of "*Matabubalah*". To which you would reply, "What's a *Matabubalah*?" (This is an old Yiddish joke. You ask your 8-year-old grandchild "would you prefer a bagel or a matabubalah?", when she replies, "what's a matabubalah?" you say, "nothing chickalah!")

I am not the first to point out this fallacy. Sam Harris got there first. Sam Harris is an American author, philosopher, neuroscientist, blogger and podcast host. He is a critic of religion and proponent of the liberty to criticize religion. He is described as one of the "Four Horsemen of New Atheism", with Richard Dawkins, Christopher Hitchens and Daniel Dennett. Yet he has this to say about the accusation that he is an atheist on his blog.

> *Atheism is not a philosophy; it is not even a view of the world; it is simply a refusal to deny the obvious. Unfortunately, we live in a world in which the obvious is overlooked as a matter of principle. The obvious must be observed and re-observed and argued for. This is a thankless job. It carries with it an aura of petulance and insensitivity. It is, moreover, a job that the atheist does not want. It is worth noting that no one ever needs to identify himself as a non-astrologer or a non-alchemist. Consequently, we do not have words for people who deny the validity of these pseudo-disciplines. Likewise, atheism is a term that should not even exist. Atheism is nothing more than the noises reasonable people make when in the presence of religious dogma.*

I think this book might be interpreted as the noise reasonable people make in the presence of religious dogma. Yet saying that I'm an atheist is like saying I'm an "*anti-matabubalist*". I would like to think that I'm more than that. Also, let me remind you, I scored more than 50% on the DSES scale and I don't think that religion is *all* bad. "Oh, no my Lord, I assure you that parts of it are excellent," said the curate to the bishop in the iconic cartoon in Punch.

TRUE HUMILITY.

*Right Reverend Host.* "I'M AFRAID YOU'VE GOT A BAD EGG, MR. JONES!"
*The Curate.* "OH NO, MY LORD, I ASSURE YOU! PARTS OF IT ARE EXCELLENT!"

These circular arguments are becoming tiresome for me and I'm sure even more tiresome for you, dear reader. So, for the rest of the book I will use the notation favored by Jonathan Sacks; G-d. This notation is multivalent as it can be read as G d or -. God for those of faith and "god of the gaps" for the sceptics. When the faithful pray or make entreaties to G-d, they tend to tip their heads to the heaven(s). This is beautifully illustrated by the painting Tiepolo's martyrdom of St. Agatha (1756), in the State Museum, Berlin.

# Why Am I a Jew?

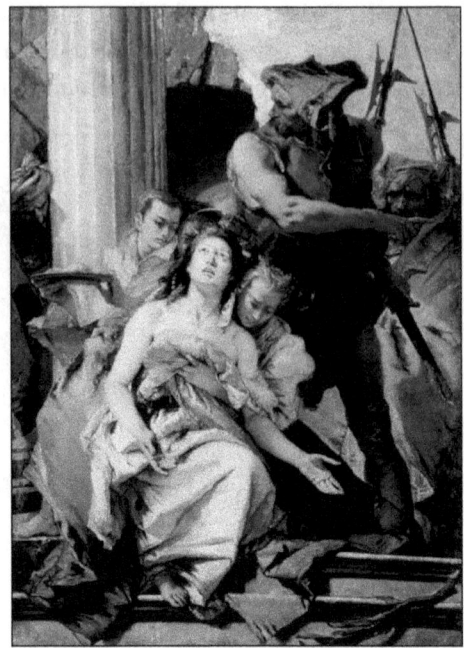

**The martyrdom of St Agatha**

Or the footballer who crosses himself as he trots on to the pitch before a big match in front of 60,000 spectators. This posture is also suggested by the psalm 121,

> "I will lift up mine eyes unto the hills, from whence cometh my help. My help cometh from the LORD, which made heaven and earth".

Heaven itself is beautifully illustrated by the starry sky in Giotto's stunning chapel in Padua. Earth is a sphere so effectively all our prayers are directed centrifugally. The nearest star, Alpha Centauri, is 4.37 light years away (5.9 trillion miles). Yet we exist in a tiny niche of the space/time continuum occupying about 70L of space and 70–80 solar years of time. As the universe expands at an estimated 67 km per second, in relative terms our niche is shrinking fast. Our expectation of life in seconds is 2,228,800,000, then by the time we die the relative position of our niche in relation

## My Search for the Divine

to the space/time horizon, will have shrunk by 67x 2.2M. These astronomical numbers are too great for our tiny brains to conceive, so we are encouraged by religious authorities to look upon ourselves as grains of sand or blades of grass (Psalm 103). This admonition to humble ourselves before G-d, out of the mouths of clerics preaching to us in gorgeous raiment, hints at hypocrisy. It reminds me of an old Jewish joke from the shtetl. Moshe was troubled, he worked hard in his tailor shop 6 days a week, was kind to his family, went to synagogue every Shabbat, but couldn't make a living and G-d never listened to his prayers. There was no rabbi in the neighborhood who he respected enough to go to for advice, but he heard of a Rabbi in the town of Chelm 20 miles away, who was both famous for his wisdom and his modesty. So, he says goodbye to his family and makes the two-day trek to Chelm, waited in a queue of other supplicants, until it is his turn to meet the great man. To his surprise the old rabbi was dressed in sackcloth and sat on a low chair. Moshe was invited to sit on a higher chair nearby. The Rabbi listened carefully without interruption to Moshe's *kvetching*, and once he was done gave some very sound advice in a quiet voice that Moshe had to strain to hear. Moshe experienced a sudden sense of enlightenment and as he stepped away, was profuse in his thanks. Just before he left the Rabbi lifted his head and said in a voice that carried to the doorway: "Nu Reb Moshe, what do you think of my modesty?"

We are not grains of dust, we are not blades of grass, we are exceptional! We are *homo sapiens,* the greatest achievement so far of G-d's creation at the point of the singularity. We are all chosen people but chosen for a purpose and carrying a burden of responsibility. Within every one of us is a "divine spark or ember" the signature of the creator. (You can read this last paragraph in two ways. The first, satisfying those who believe the creator is a supernatural entity, is a literal translation, and second satisfying those who have no belief in a supernatural entity, might recognize I'm using metaphors.)

What I'm trying to describe is my sense of awe I feel at the beauty of creation and my unconditional love for others. (I scored top marks for those two domains on the DSES scale, mind you I also scored bottom marks for my belief that G-d might love me back!).

I do not share Macbeth's pessimistic take on the meaning of life. I like to think that atheist or not, Jewish, or not, we are all chosen people, but for what purpose and for what responsibility I remain unsure? If nothing else I feel a powerful sense of responsibility for all others of my species, it's there, it's real, I don't look upon it as a virtue, it's more like a compulsion, an instinct or a gravitational pull. Am I simply describing a behavior or way of thinking that has an evolutionary advantage, if so, what anatomical site does it occupy in my brain? Is there a gland that secretes "the milk of human kindness"? Can we stimulate that organ, or does it atrophy as we grow older or through neglect? Whatever it might be let us use the shorthand and call it "love". I will now describe my reductionist search for the source of love. Much of this will involve metaphor because I don't have adequate words to describe my quest.

## A SOLIPSIST VIEW OF THE UNIVERSE

When I first heard the word, *solipsist* used in everyday speech, I had no idea what it meant but didn't want to show my ignorance. It was used to unfavorably describe a colleague who was out of the room at the time. It sounded like an onomatopoeia, meaning something slippery, that was indeed a good description of the individual. When I got home, I looked it up in the Oxford English dictionary and this is what I found:

> Solipsism, the view, or theory that the self is all that can be known to exist. -The quality of being self-centered or selfish.

So, in practice it carries two meanings, the first describing a philosophy and the second describing an unattractive personality. The word is indeed slippery because someone who subscribes to the philosophy doesn't necessarily have to be self-centered and selfish. I wish to take that word and embellish it with another meaning because I cannot find an alternative that can be used as a shorthand for what I'm about to describe.

I hope you understood my argument that nothing outside our solar system can have any relevance within our tiny space/time niche. Those of a religious bent might argue, "What about dark matter?" This makes for an expedient way of buttressing their beliefs and implies the existence of God as an amorphous something that is omniscient, omnipotent and listens to our prayers in dark matter. For the sceptics, this is yet an example of the G-d of the gaps. I have no problem with those who find solace and comfort in directing their prayers to dark matter, but it is difficult to believe that dark matter is the source of love when it has stood by as a silent witness of the utmost savagery of man on man, over the last three millennia. You can't have it both ways. I would therefore politely ask you to consider looking inwards for the divine source of love, let your hopes and prayers reverse their direction from the centrifugal directions of outer space to the centripetal direction of inner space. This is the concept I'm trying to grasp that adds another meaning to the word solipsism. Think upon ourselves as a solar system. We are indeed the sun at the center of our micro-universe. We are circled by planets, our children, who in turn or in time will be circled by their moons, our grandchildren. Every individual in our own micro-universe will in turn become a solar system, where we, the grandparents, will become distant orbiting planets and their children will become the closest of their orbiting worlds. The hypothetical model becomes more and more complex, like Venn diagrams superimposed one upon the other, until we discover that everyone who ever lived is related to everyone who is alive today.

Let us now return to our solipsist selves and consider the properties of a sun. Our sun, quite modest in size compared to *Proxima Centauri*, radiates energy that keeps us warm and provides the bombardment of photons to allow for photosynthesis that provides us with our food. This entity is not self-centered or selfish. You would have to look further afield for an entity like that, and I'm talking about black holes. The closest black hole we know of is V616 Monocerotis, and located about 3,000 light years away, and has between 9–13 times the mass of the Sun. Taking the analogy further we now have a model or metaphor for distinguishing good from evil. Goodness and virtue are the human properties of nurturing and cherishing all those in your orbit. We do this not for reward but because it is in our nature. We expect nothing in return other than the *hope* of reciprocation. Evil is represented by the properties of a black hole. A black hole has a boundary, called the event horizon. It is where gravity is just strong enough to drag light back and prevent it escaping. Because nothing can travel faster than light, everything else will get dragged back also. There are ideologies of the past and the present, that behave like black holes, and it is our duty to protect the vulnerable of our specious from getting too close. Like Icarus they will lose more than their wings.

Continuing with my allegory; how do we generate our radiant heat, where do we search for this divine spark, this ember left over from the big bang? When physiologists discuss the working of the Central Nervous System (CNS) they describe afferent and efferent pathways. Afferent means stimuli conducted inwards and efferent; stimuli conducted outwards. The sensory nerve receptors for, sight, sound, smell, touch and taste conduct stimuli into specific region of the cerebral cortex that responds in with an appropriate cascade of efferent signals to the mind or to the sympathetic and parasympathetic end organs. Fearful sights and sounds may provoke the sympathetic neural network to trigger a fright or fight response. Delightful smells and tastes provoke the nerves to the salivary glands to make your mouth water. A touch in the dark when you think you are alone might provoke fear whereas the same touch might provoke delight when you are in bed with your lover. What then provokes the sensation of love? You recognize love when you feel it but must rely on conceptual metaphors to describe it. Here are three examples almost lifted at random.

# My Search for the Divine

## A Star

> Love is an ever-fixed mark
> That looks on tempests and is never shaken;
> It is the star to every wandering bark,
> Whose worth's unknown, although his height be taken.
> (William Shakespeare, Sonnet 116, 1609)

## A Key

> Love is the master key that unlocks the gates of happiness,
> of hatred, of jealousy, and most easily of all, the gate of fear.
> (Oliver Wendell Holmes, A Moral Antipathy, 1885)

## A Spark

> Yes, love indeed is light from heaven;
> A spark of that immortal fire.
> With angels shared, by Alla given,
> To lift from earth our low desire.
> (Lord Byron, The Giaour, 1813)

There are literally hundreds of examples from prose and poetry I could have used to illustrate the point I'm making. My favorite is the third, composed by Lord Byron, because it allows me to continue with my own analogy of a divine spark that is a gift of G-d or in this case Alla *(sic)*. It also allows for a concept of love that is more than sexual desire. The afferent stimulus is recognition of the loved one through one or more of the five senses. What then goes on in the brain is too complex to imagine and the gland that "secretes the milk of human kindness" must be separate to the gland that provokes sexual arousal. The latter is well researched, but the former is at the frontier of neurophysiological research. I have faith in my clever colleagues that one day they will unravel the threads of *this* rainbow, but for me that is a step too far. It does no harm to leave room for mystery and romanticism and I believe that the same "gland" that inspires the greatest works of art, music, literature, and painting, bridges the gap with the gland for both sexual desire and filial love. What goes on in the brain when enjoying you visit to a great art gallery, what neuroactive polypeptides are released to produce this pleasant feeling? This can be studied and has been studied. I once attended a conference on the links between science an art and remember a very clever experiment that was demonstrated. A volunteer was invited to sit before a large screen and wired up for measuring skin temperature, blood pressure, sweating and an electroencephalogram. The screen then generated at random, colors and shapes whilst the volunteer was monitored. The volunteer was invited to stop the image when he found it most pleasing. To my eye this produced some acceptable abstract art that corresponded with physiological measurements suggesting low sympathetic activity and high para-sympathetic activity that in human terms corresponds to a nice sense of warm relaxation or nirvana. Yet the mystery and romanticism associated with making and viewing art was lost, a reductionist step too far for my taste. To live a good life and a life of virtue, all that's asked of us is to experience love, activate love and use that *spark of immortal fire* to warm and nurture those in our orbits. We don't need to understand the mechanisms, but others are free to continue the search. For the time being and for simple convenience let us call that *spark of immortal fire* dancing away in the gland of human kindness, "The Soul". This will please those with religious beliefs who have stuck with me to the end yet should not deter my scientific friends from exploring these outer reaches of our mind. As a scientist searching for the soul, I suggest that we dilute the human body just beyond Avogadro's constant, $6 \times 10^{-23}$, that then enters the zone of granularity, somewhere in that nothingness we will find the G-d particle or ember. Maybe our centripetal prayers act like a gentle zephyr that keeps the home fire burning.

THE END

# *Bibliography*

Alimujiang A et al, *Association Between Life Purpose and Mortality Among US Adults Older Than 50 Years*. JAMA Netw Open.;2(5):e194270. 2019.

Bartholomew, Robert E.; Wessely, *"Protean nature of mass sociogenic illness: From possessed nuns to chemical and biological terrorism fears"*. British Journal of Psychiatry. Royal College of Psychiatrists. 180 (4): 300–306, 2002.

Browne, T, *The Works of Sir Thomas Brown, Religio Medici*. London, George Bell & Sons, 1901.

Browne, T, *The Works of Sir Thomas Browne, Vulgar Errors*. London, George Bell & Sons, 1901.

Cook H, *Western Medicine: an illustrated History, From the Scientific Revolution to the Germ Theory*. Edited by Irvine Lonudon, Oxford, Oxford University Press, 1997.

Dawkins, R, *The Blind Watchmaker*. Penguin, Random House, UK, 2016.

Dawkins, Richard, *Richard Dawkins perplexed by high numbers of Jewish Nobel Prize winners*. The Algemeiner, October2 9th, 2013.

Freedman, H. *Reason to believe, The Louis Jacobs Affair*. London, Published by Bloomsbury Continuum, 2021.

Gray, RH, Kigozi G, Serwadda D, et al. *Male circumcision for HIV prevention in men in Rakai, Uganda: a randomised trial*. The Lancet; 369:657-666.2007.

Hammer MF, Behar DM, Karafet TM et al, *Extended Y chromosome haplotypes resolve multiple and unique lineages of the Jewish priesthood*; 126 (5):707-17. 2009

https://www.algemeiner.com/2013/10/29/richard-dawkins-perplexed-by-high-number-of-jewish-nobel-prize-winners/

Hawking S, *A brief history of time: from big bangs to black holes*. Bantam Dell Publishing Group, New York, NY, p256, 1988

Idler E, Blevins J, Kiser M and Hogue C, *Religion, a social determinant of mortality? A 10-year follow-up of the Health and Retirement Study*. 2017. PLoS ONE 12(12): e0189134. https://doi. org/10.1371/journal.pone.0189134

# BIBLIOGRAPHY

Kazi TB and Naidoo S; *Does Religiosity Mediate Suicidal Tendencies? A South African Study of Muslim Tertiary Students.* J Relig Health.;55(3):1010-1023. 2016.

Lem S, *Chance and Order.* The New Yorker 59, 30 January 88-98. 1984.

Levy-Ahad E, Catane R, Eisenberg S, et al *Founder BRCA1 and BRCA2 mutations in Ashkenazi Jews in Israel: frequency and differential penetrance in ovarian cancer and in breast-ovarian cancer families.* Am J Hum Genet. 60(5): 1059–1067, 1997.

Marmot M. *Social determinants of health inequalities.* The Lancet, Volume 365, Issue 9464, 19–25, 1005-1006, 2005.

Montaigne M, *Essays, translated by JM Cohen.* London, Penguin, Random House, 1988.

Nadler, S, *A book forged in hell.* Princeton University Press, Princeton, 2011.

Nadler, Steven. *A book forged in Hell.* Princeton: Princeton University Press, 2011.

Nurbakhsh, J, *Discourses on the Sufi path.* Google books, 1996.

Popper, K, *Conjectures and Refutations.* Routledge, London & New York, First Published 1963, reprinted 2000.

Priestman T, Baum M, Jones V, Forbes J. *Treatment and survival in advanced breast cancer.* Br Med J 2:1673-1674, 1978.

Priestman TJ, Baum M. *Evaluation of quality of life in patients receiving treatment for advanced breast cancer.* Lancet i:899-901, 1976.

Rosen S. *Physiological insights into Shechita.* The Veterinary Record; 154,759-765, 2004.

Rutherford, A, *A Brief History of everyone who ever lived.* London, Weidenfeld & Nicolson, 2017.

Ryff CD and Keyes CLM. *The structure of psychological well-being revisited.* J Pers Soc Psychol;69(4):719-727. 1995.

Sacks J, http://rabbisacks.org/covenant-conversation-5768-ki-tavo-the-blessing-and-the-curse/. 2008.

Schama, S. *Belonging: The story of the Jews 1492-1900.* The Bodley Head, London, 200, 2017

Schama, S. *Belonging: The story of the Jews 1492-1900.* The Bodley Head, London, 206-207, 2017.

Scruton R, *Spinoza, A very short introduction.* Oxford University Press, Oxford, 2002.

Sheremer, M, *The Science of Good and Evil.* New York: Times Books, 2004.

Siegel-Itzkovich, J, *Gene tests show that two fifths of Ashkenazi Jews are descended from four women.* BMJ, 140, 332(7534): 2006.

Steinberg M. *As a driven Leaf.* 1939, Republished by Behrman House, Springfield, NJ, 2015

Taleb, NN. *The Black Swan.* Penguin Books, London 2008.

Taub Centre Staff Bulletin, *Live Long and Prosper: Health in the Haredi Community.* May 31, 2016.

# BIBLIOGRAPHY

Underwood, LG, *The Daily Spiritual Experience Scale: Overview and Results.* Religions, 2(1), 29-50; 2011.

Voltaire: *Philosophical Dictionary, translated by Theodore Besterman.* London, Penguin Classics, 1972.

Wilchek-Aviad Y, Malka M, *Religiosity, Meaning in Life and Suicidal Tendency Among Jews.* Journal of Religious Health;55(2):480-94. 2016.

# *Index*

## A

Abraham, 14
Alexander, Cecil, 5
anthropocentric, 2
Arab, 58, 86, 87, 90, 91, 93
Aristotle, 108
Auster, Paul, 1

## B

Baum, Professor David, 64
Bor, Dr Harris, 112
Browne, Thomas, 18

## C

C.P. Snow, x
Chanukah, 62
Charedim, 67, 69, 120
Christian, 11, 34, 42, 44, 45, 107, 115, 117, 130
chromosomes, 3
community, 15, 38, 40, 43–46, 52–54, 63, 64, 70, 80, 100, 102
cosmos, xi, 2

## D

Darwin, Charles, 5, 55
Dawkins, Richard 10, 18, 21, 39, 59, 134
DNA, 3, 10, 51
Druze, 91

## E

eruv, 66
eugenics, 16, 31
Exodus, 6, 12, 63, 71, 78

## G

genes, 3, 15, 50
God, ix, x, xi, 2, 5, 6, 9–16, 19–20, 25–26, 28–29, 32–33, 35, 39, 41–42, 44, 49, 57–58, 64, 67, 69–70, 72–73, 102–103, 102–103, 106–107, 109–112, 116–119, 122, 132, 135, 139
Goldilocks fallacy, 4

## H

Hawking, Stephen 2

# INDEX

Heaven, 34, 35, 47, 60, 64, 94, 101, 107, 135, 136
Hell, 6, 34, 35, 47, 101, 112, 117
Hitchins, Christopher, 18, 21, 39, 134
Hitler, 30, 49, 86
holistic, 2
holistic hierarchy, 3
holocaust, 12, 25, 31, 85–89, 90, 113
holon, 3
Homo Sapiens, 9, 10, 13, 15, 50, 72, 130
Hume, David, 109

## I

Islam, 16, 27, 28
Israel, 23, 41, 46, 49, 53, 55, 58, 62, 69, 77, 79, 85, 87, 88, 90, 92, 115

## J

Jacobs, Rabbi Lewi, 6
Jakobovits, Lord Immanuel, 18
Jerusalem, 24, 40, 41, 42, 68, 86, 88, 89, 121, 126
Johnson, Samuel xii

## K

Kant, 18, 21, 57
Kosher, 62, 65, 72, 74, 76, 77, 79–81

## L

Leviticus, 61, 76, 81, 94, 99, 100
Liss, Rabbi, 60

## M

Maimonides 18, 71, 82, 109 119
meaning of life, 2, 38, 123–125, 138
medical humanities, x
Michel de Montaigne, 18–20
moral philosophy, x, 13, 17, 33, 59, 60, 101
Moses, xi, 6, 15, 27, 28, 33, 51, 77, 81, 82, 106
misogyny, 34, 38, 101

## N

Nadler, Steven, 117
Nazi, 30, 31, 50, 85, 90, 91, 114, 117
Newton, Issac 5, 20, 97
nucleus, 3

## O

ontology, x, 108
Orwell, George, 32

## P

Palestine, 89, 115
Passover, 26, 62, 71, 79
Pesach, 62, 71
Popper, Karl, 18, 21, 61, 108

## R

Rosh Hashanah, 6, 62

## S

Sacks, Jonathan 12, 13, 26, 54, 123, 135
scientific philosophy, 34

# INDEX

Scruton, Roger, 18
Shabbat, 60, 63–65, 67, 68, 114, 137
shul, 68
spider, 1, 2, 34
Spinoza, 6, 9, 12, 18, 19, 21, 105–112, 116, 117, 119, 120, 122
Sukkot, 62
supernatural, ix, 13–15, 18, 118, 137
synagogue, 52–55, 60, 61, 65–68, 79, 114, 120, 137

## T

Taleb, Nassim, 109
Torah, 63

## U

Uroboros, 4

## V

Voltaire, 18, 21, 30, 34

## W

Wesley, Sir Simon, 31
Winston, Lord Robert, 60

## Y

Yad Vashem, 89, 90
Yom Kippur, 6, 61, 62, 66

## Z

Zionist, 49, 84, 85

www.ingramcontent.com/pod-product-compliance
Lightning Source LLC
Chambersburg PA
CBHW050823160426
43192CB00010B/1871